Albert Camus

Personal Writings

Albert Camus was born in Algeria in 1913. He spent the early years of his life in North Africa, where he became a journalist. During the Nazi occupation of France, his essential contributions to the underground newspaper *Combat* and the publication of *The Stranger* and *The Myth of Sisyphus* established him as a beacon of the Resistance in postwar intellectual life. His fiction, including *The Stranger, The Plague, The Fall,* and *Exile and the Kingdom;* his philosophical essays, *The Myth of Sisyphus* and *The Rebel;* and his plays have assured his preeminent position in modern letters. In 1957, Camus was awarded the Nobel Prize in Literature. On January 4, 1960, he was killed in a car accident.

INTERNATIONAL

Personal
Writings

Personal Writings

Albert Camus

Translated from the French by
Ellen Conroy Kennedy and Justin O'Brien

With a Foreword by Alice Kaplan

VINTAGE INTERNATIONAL
VINTAGE BOOKS
A DIVISION OF PENGUIN RANDOM HOUSE LLC
NEW YORK

Contents

Foreword

Alice Kaplan

Albert Camus is one of the few French writers of the last century to have emerged from genuine hardship. Born to a deaf, illiterate mother and a father killed in the Battle of the Marne when Camus was eleven months old, he was raised in a barren apartment in Belcourt, a working-class neighborhood of Algiers. *The Wrong Side and the Right Side*, *Nuptials*, and *Summer*, gathered here in a newly organized collection titled *Personal Writings*, speak from his emotional core about these beginnings and provide the foundation for all his work to come. For Americans who know Camus only through the hard-boiled prose of *The Stranger*, the lush emotional intensity of these early essays and stories will come as a surprise.

It is exciting, too, to discover here, in poetic form, the underpinnings of Camus's philosophical thought. In *The Wrong Side and the Right Side*, he gleans "the whole *absurd* simplicity of the world" as he sits with his silent, indifferent mother, incapable of understanding her. Here is the germ of the absurd condition he defines in *The Myth of Sisyphus*: the idea that the world will always dash our attempts to make meaning. Camus will argue in his later works that to be lucid in the face of death yet tend to the fate of the living, or, like Sisyphus, to push a rock up a hill only to see it fall back down and begin again with a sense of joy at the impossible task, is a form of revolt against our condition. In "The Enigma" (*Summer*) he writes, "Where is the absurdity of the world? . . . I should like, faced with the white and black clarity that, for me, has always been the sign of truth, to explain in simple terms what I feel about this absurdity which I know too well to allow anyone to hold forth on it without making certain nuances." By now he has grown impatient with his reputation as a bard of the absurd. But in his earliest essays, *The Wrong Side and the Right Side* and *Nuptials*, he is still dancing around meaning, ready to embrace what he hasn't yet put into words. And especially in the essays where he explores the physical universe, we can sense the beginnings of his commitment to "measure" or "equilibrium," to the truth that comes from the confrontation of black and white. He argues through image and metaphor and produces something like a maxim for a philosophy in the making when he writes in "Return to Tipasa": "In the depths of winter, I finally learned that within me there lay an invincible summer." Later, in his essay *The Rebel,* Camus will call this measured vision of the world "thought at the Meridian."

The Wrong Side and the Right Side and *Nuptials* were published in Algiers in 1937 and 1939; Camus's debut made an impact among a small group of writers in Algeria but was scarcely noticed in France. In 1957, after he had become a renowned writer, his French publisher reissued *The Wrong Side and the Right Side.* In a preface to the new edition, he still referred to his first writings as "feeble testimony," yet his belief in their value was absolute:

> Every artist keeps within himself a single source which nourishes during his lifetime what he is and what he says. When that spring runs dry, little by little one sees his work shrivel and crack. . . . As for myself, I know that my source is in *The Wrong Side and the Right Side,* in the world of poverty and sunlight I lived in for so long, whose memory still saves me from two opposing dangers that threaten every artist, resentment and self-satisfaction.

Perhaps it was his weariness over the philosophical and political battles in Paris that made him long to re-create what he had achieved in his very first book: "If, in spite of so many efforts to create a language and bring myths to life, I never manage to rewrite *The Wrong Side and the Right Side,* I shall have achieved nothing. I feel this in my bones."

He would return often to this intuitive understanding of his art, where the least practiced writing became, in retrospect, his benchmark.

What once might have seemed awkward to Camus in *The Wrong Side and the Right Side*, *Nuptials*, and *Summer*—the abrupt transitions, the indirect allusions, the taste for maxims—has stood the test of time. Magically lyrical, moving from abstract philosophy to poetry, and driven by anguish and pleasure, they don't correspond to any set genre. They are unpredictable, unique literary wonders, even more meaningful when read together.

The Wrong Side and the Right Side

L'Envers et l'Endroit is a hard title to translate. In French, it can refer to the two sides of a piece of fabric—the one on which you sew and the underside, or the two sides of a coin, heads and tails. *The Wrong Side and the Right Side* consists of five short pieces organized around an ambiguity, a neither/nor-ness.

"Irony" shows how deeply and surprisingly Camus grasped the misery of old age when he was only in his twenties. The essay begins with the days and hours in the life of a very old woman and a very old man. A concluding section describes a family that resembles Camus's own: a silent mother and uncle, two sons, and a mean grandmother—a childhood world he chose as the setting for *The First Man*, his last posthumously published novel. In this early sketch, the grandmother is a fake and a bully who makes her grandson say he likes her better than his own mother. She vomits theatrically, and on her deathbed, she farts like a pig. At her funeral, the grandson, the ancestor of

Meursault in *The Stranger*, refuses to kowtow to society's pressures: "He was afraid of being insincere and telling lies in the presence of death." In the conclusion, Camus admits that the three parts of his essay don't fit together very well. But neither, he adds, do the sorrow and radiance of the world.

In "Between Yes and No," Camus grapples with his childhood. A man spends the evening in a Moorish café in the upper Casbah where he can see the lights along the Bay of Algiers. He is flooded with memories of the apartment where he grew up with his mother and grandmother: the banister he dreaded because of cockroaches, the working men on the balconies across the street, the sound of the tramway. His mother is deaf. She stares out from her balcony, thinking of nothing. The writer cries out, "The indifference of this strange mother! Only the solitude of the world can be the measure of it." This mother is inexplicable, and the child's love for her is boundless. "The bizarre feeling a son has for his mother constitutes *his entire sensibility*," Camus wrote in his work-in-progress notebooks around this time. In *The Stranger*, begun two years later, Meursault is indifferent to his mother. And from the solitary indifference of his own mother, so strongly evoked here, Camus created Meursault's indifference.

"Death in the Soul" is a primer for solitary travel. A man finds himself in a hotel in Prague with barely enough money to live. He orders a greasy goulash drowning in cumin and retreats to his hotel room only to discover that another guest, a total stranger, has died in an adjoining room. "Any country where I am not bored is a country that teaches me nothing," he decides, then mocks his pompous homily. "That was the kind of remark I tried out to cheer myself up." After this grim tale comes "Love of Life," inspired by another trip to his mother's ancestral Balearic Islands in 1935. The story begins in a cabaret in Palma and offers Camus a happier occasion to reflect on the powers of looking and enjoying that come with travel. A year later, the Spanish Republic began its losing battle against Franco. Despite his deep affinities for the Spanish landscape and people, Camus refused to return to a fascist Spain.

In the title story, "The Wrong Side and the Right Side," placed last in the collection, an old woman purchases a funeral vault and has her name inscribed on the tomb. Every Sunday, she travels to the cemetery and kneels beside her own grave. "And now I think about these things again," Camus writes, in one of the guileless transitions that makes these essays both abstract and intimate. Looking out his window on a January day, enjoying the shadows of branches on his white curtains, he, too, is "face-to-face with the wrong side of the world."

The bleakness and despair but also the gallows humor in *The Wrong Side and the Right Side* were the product of a period in Camus's life marked by illness and marital troubles. His first wife, Simone Hié, was a morphine addict, and the trip to Central Europe he describes in "Death in the Soul" was based on the trip he began with her, until he discovered she had been sleeping with a doctor who supplied her with drugs. He doesn't write explicitly about their separation: it can scarcely be glimpsed beneath his solitude. Nor does he mention his ongoing struggle with tuberculosis, contracted at age seventeen, which brought him into close conversation with death and affected everything he wrote.

Nuptials

In 1937, when Edmond Charlot published *The Wrong Side and the Right Side*, Camus was already working on four new essays or stories that would become *Nuptials*. At first glance, *Nuptials* portrays a different world from the one explored in the previous volume: poverty and despair give way to a joyous communion with nature. Between the first book and the second, Camus's life had changed. His unhappy marriage had ended. He was expelled from the Algerian Communist Party as a dissident. He had founded a new theater troupe. In 1937, the writer and actor spent his days with a couple of friends, Marguerite Dubrenn and Jeanne Sicard, and a new lover, Christiane Galindo, in the bungalow they dubbed "The House Above the World," with its magnificent view of the Bay of Algiers and the mountains beyond.

The first essay in *Nuptials*, "Nuptials at Tipasa," remains the most famous of all of Camus's personal writings, and it has always had a special status in Algeria. Today if you travel to the ruins in the village of Tipasa, forty-two miles west of Algiers, you're likely to see fellow visitors carrying a paperback of *Nuptials* or reading out loud among the stones. The archaeological site contains several layers of civilization: an old Phoenician port and trading center; a Roman colony; a center of fervent early Christianity, named after its patron, Saint Salsa, martyred by pagans. Camus barely dwells on the history of the place. In "Nuptials at Tipasa," he honors the Mediterranean. As a young communist speaking at the Algiers cultural center, Camus argued—already defining himself against the rigidity of the party—for a liberating relationship to the landscape: "What we claim as Mediterranean is not a liking for reasoning and abstractions, but its physical life—the courtyard, the cypresses, the strings of pimientos."*

But no matter how sunny, how alive, his portrait of Tipasa in *Nuptials*, joy for Camus is always coupled with despair. "There is no love of life without despair of life," he writes in "Love of Life." The phrase captures something essential: Camus referred many times to the unfathomable fact that his childhood was both impoverished and happy. What attracted Camus to Tipasa is also a paradox: a "kingdom of ruins" where culture has reverted to nature through the process of natural decay. In the basilica, sage and wildflowers grow where there used to be corpses. And in the great tradition of the nineteenth-century Romantics, the ruin is the privileged site for love, "a marriage of ruins and springtime." Amorous gestures transfer from lovers to the world of things: "crushing absinthe leaves, caressing ruins, matching my breathing with the world's tumultuous sighs." Breath in Camus's writing is never neutral. His lungs were slowly decaying, and he didn't expect to grow old.

*"La culture indigène: La nouvelle culture méditerranéenne" (1937) in *Conférences et discours*.

"Nuptials in Tipasa" is followed by "The Wind at Djemila." Camus traveled to Djemila, an archaeological site in the northeastern mountains of Kabylia, in an airplane owned by his friend Marie Viton. That escapade is nowhere here. A dry, windy, and foreboding place, the village of Djemila becomes an occasion to meditate on death, on the blue of the sky, on the punishing wind, and especially on illness. Camus rails at death, setting a scene he must have lived and witnessed in the tubercular ward at Mustapha Hospital: "You can be lying in bed one day and hear someone say: 'You are strong and I owe it to you to be honest: I can tell you that you are going to die'; you're there, with your whole life in your hands, fear in your bowels, looking the fool. What else matters: waves of blood come throbbing to my temples and I feel I could smash everything around me."

"Summer in Algiers," as joyous as "The Wind at Djemila" is stark, flows over with movie houses, dance halls, swimming spots, countless idiotic amusements, and a sense of wonder about his hometown: "What is so unique in these fleeting evenings of Algiers that they free so many things in me?" In the final essay, "The Desert," written under the sign of Giotto and De la Francesca and based on memories of his own Italian sojourns in 1936 and 1937, Camus draws still more lessons for living from the landscape and the people of Tuscany. Here his focus wanders, until he can't decide if he is really writing about Italy or about the eternal quest for balance—between yes and no, happiness and bitterness, asceticism and sensuality.

Summer

The third collection included here is the longest of the three and the most diffuse, with the earliest essay dated 1939 and the latest 1953.

Camus began to write "The Minotaur" after moving to Oran in 1939. His newspaper, *Alger Républicain*, had just been shut down by a reactionary government. Finding himself without resources, he was forced to leave Algiers for Oran, where he moved in with the family of his fiancée, Francine Faure, in their apartment on the Rue d'Arzew in the commercial center. Oran annoyed him. He claimed that the city turned in on itself like a snail, snubbing the sea—that it was nothing but dusty stones. In the town square known as the Place d'Armes, two ridiculous bronze lions graced the steps of the city hall. Camus delighted in recounting the legend: they were said to trot out onto the square every night to relieve themselves.

Camus's editor in Algiers planned to publish "The Minotaur" in a chapbook in 1942, but it was censored by the Vichy government, who had other plans for a quickly dwindling supply of paper. So Camus waited and published the essay in one of the little magazines that sprang up in Algiers at the liberation. Seven years later, he included it in *Summer*. By then he had taken his antipathy for Oran even further: he had set a fictional plague in the city, in a novel about which he liked to say ruefully that it had more victims than he could have anticipated. *The Plague* was Camus's first great commercial success. For readers of *The Plague*, "The Minotaur" is a fascinating warm-up—

scales for the work to come. *The Plague* gave him such a bad reputation in Oran that he wrote a mock apology in the form of a heavily ironic headnote to "The Minotaur": "Violent protests emanating from this beautiful town have in fact assured me that all the imperfections have been (or will be) remedied."

Though it has a more disenchanted voice than *Nuptials*, *Summer* is *Nuptials*'s heir. Camus is still exploring the shades of despair and joy in nature. If you can make it through the coldest night in February, he says in "The Almond Trees," you'll wake up to those almond trees in bloom. In "The Enigma," he casts a bitter glance at the Parisian literary scene. Other essays in *Summer* speak to his deepest values: "Helen's Exile" extolls the Greek sense of measure—an argument he would return to in *The Rebel*. In "A Short Guide to Towns Without a Past," he delights in making fun of the rivalry between Oran and Algiers by way of boxing matches—the equivalent of a Yankees–Red Sox series. In "The Sea Close By," he uses a boat trip in South America to explore his eternal sense of exile.

In 1953, after Camus had been living full-time in Paris for nearly a decade, he returned to Tipasa. It was December, it had been raining for five days, and the air was so humid you could almost drink it, he said. What had become of the sunlight that had once devoured everything? In 1939, when he published *Nuptials*, Camus was unknown beyond his circle in Algiers. The man who returned to Tipasa in 1953 was the author of *The Stranger*, the bestselling *Plague*, the essays *The Myth of Sisyphus* and *The Rebel*, as well as several well-known plays. He was a famous man. Europe was now in its own state of ruin. European intellectuals were being torn apart by debates over communism. Sartre and Camus had fallen out over Camus's attack on Marxism in *The Rebel*. The exchange had taken place publicly in Sartre's magazine *Les Temps Modernes* and had become so bitter as to leave no room for reconciliation. Tipasa, too, had changed: there was barbed wire surrounding the site, and you needed authorization to enter. It was no longer a natural spot for lovers. Yet by attending to the sky, the air, and the light, the forty-year-old writer regained access to the Algerian wellspring that would allow him to confront the dark night of injustice in Europe. Like an artist returning to his sketchbook, Camus looked to Tipasa—the place and the memory—as an ever-available source of renewal.

Today in Tipasa, if you walk past the ruins along a cliff high above the Mediterranean, you will find the only memorial to Camus in all of Algeria. Inscribed on a simple block of stone, faded from the wind and barely legible, is this single line from "Nuptials at Tipasa": "Here I understand what is meant by glory: the right to love without limits."

These personal essays address a central question of identity: Was Camus Algerian or French? Camus's education in French schools, his French publisher in Paris, and an adult life spent in the intellectual hothouse of Saint-Germain-des-Prés all mark him as a consummate French writer. And yet it's a mistake not to take into account everything he owes to his Algerian childhood, so beautifully rendered here. While he was following a French intellectual tradition, his birthplace infuses the images he uses and the texture of his work. Today, many Algerian writers claim him as part of their literary tradition. And this is the case despite the harsh critiques he's received for the flatness, even the namelessness of Arab characters in his fiction. In a speech he gave in Paris in 1958, Camus expressed in the strongest terms what Algeria had meant to him. He referred to the group of French and native writers in the "School of Algiers" united around Edmond Charlot's small publishing house. He said that having been born in Algeria was the greatest good fortune of his existence. And, once again, he repeated his literary credo: "I've never written anything that isn't directly or indirectly tied to this land."*

---

*"*J'ai eu l'occasion de dire que je n'avais rien écrit qui, de près ou de loin, ne se rattache à cette terre.*" Speech to the Algerienne Association, November 13, 1958, in *Conférences et discours.*

I

The Wrong Side
and the Right Side

1937

(*L'Envers et l'Endroit*)

to Jean Grenier

Preface, 1958

The essays collected in this volume were written in 1935 and 1936 (I was then twenty-two) and published a year later in Algeria in a very limited edition. This edition has been unobtainable for a long time and I have always refused to have *The Wrong Side and the Right Side* reprinted.

There are no mysterious reasons for my stubbornness. I reject nothing of what these writings express, but their form has always seemed clumsy to me. The prejudices on art I cherish in spite of myself (I shall explain them further on) kept me for a long time from considering their republication. A great vanity, it would seem, leading one to suppose that my other writings satisfy every standard. Need I say this isn't so? I am only more aware of the inadequacies in *The Wrong Side and the Right Side* than of those in my other work. How can I explain this except by admitting that these inadequacies concern and reveal the subject closest to my heart. The question of its literary value settled, then, I can confess that for me this little book has considerable value as testimony. I say for me, since it is to me that it reveals and from me that it demands a fidelity whose depth and difficulties I alone can know. I should like to try to explain why.

Brice Parain often maintains that this little book contains my best work. He is wrong. I do not say this, knowing how honest he is, because of the impatience every artist feels when people are impertinent enough to prefer what he has been to what he is. No, he is wrong because at twenty-two, unless one is a genius, one scarcely knows how to write. But I understand what Parain, learned enemy of art and philosopher of compassion, is trying to say. He means, and he is right, that there is more love in these awkward pages than in all those that have followed.

Every artist thus keeps within himself a single source which nourishes during his lifetime what he is and what he says. When that spring runs dry, little by little one sees his work shrivel and crack. These are art's wastelands, no longer watered by the invisible current. His hair grown thin and dry, covered with thatch, the artist is ripe for silence or the salons, which comes to the same thing. As for myself, I know that my source is in *The Wrong Side and the Right Side,* in the world of poverty and sunlight I lived in for so long, whose memory still saves me from two opposing dangers that threaten every artist, resentment and self-satisfaction.

Poverty, first of all, was never a misfortune for me: it was radiant with light. Even my revolts were brilliant with sunshine. They were almost always, I think I can say this without hypocrisy, revolts for everyone, so that every life might be lifted into that light. There is no certainty my heart was naturally disposed to this kind of love. But circumstances helped me. To correct a natural indifference, I was placed halfway between poverty and the sun. Poverty kept me from thinking all was well under the sun and in history; the sun taught me that history was not everything. I wanted to change lives, yes, but not the world which I worshipped as divine. I suppose this is how I got started on my present difficult career, innocently stepping onto the tightrope upon which I move painfully forward, unsure of reaching the end. In other words, I became an artist, if it is true that there is no art without refusal or consent.

In any case, the lovely warmth that reigned over my childhood freed me from all resentment. I lived on almost nothing, but also in a kind of rapture. I felt infinite strengths within me: all I had to do was find a way to use them. It was not poverty that got in my way: in Africa, the sun and the sea cost nothing. The obstacle lay rather in prejudices or stupidity. These gave me every opportunity to develop a "Castilian pride" that has done me much harm, that my friend and teacher Jean Grenier is right to make fun of, and that I tried in vain to correct, until I realized that there is a fatality in human natures. It seemed better to accept my pride and try to make use of it, rather than give myself, as Chamfort would put it, principles stronger than my character. After some soul-searching, however, I can testify that among my many weaknesses I have never discovered that most widespread failing, envy, the true cancer of societies and doctrines.

I take no credit for so fortunate an immunity. I owe it to my family, first of all, who lacked almost everything and envied practically nothing. Merely by their silence, their reserve, their natural sober pride, my people, who did not even know how to read, taught me the most valuable and enduring lessons. Anyhow, I was too absorbed in feeling to dream of things. Even now, when I see the life of the very rich in Paris, there is compassion in the detachment it inspires in me. One finds many injustices in the world, but there is one that is never mentioned, climate. For a long time, without realizing it, I thrived on that particular injustice. I can imagine the accusations of our grim philanthropists, if they should happen to read these lines. I want to pass the workers off as rich and the bourgeois as poor, to prolong the happy servitude of the former and the power of the latter. No, that is not it. For the final and most revolting injustice is consummated when poverty is wed to the life without hope or the sky that I found on reaching manhood in the appalling slums of our cities: everything must be done so that men can escape from the double humiliation of poverty and ugliness. Though born poor in a working-class neighborhood, I never knew what real misfortune was until I saw our chilling suburbs. Even extreme Arab poverty cannot be compared to it, because of the difference in climate. But anyone who has known these industrial slums feels forever soiled, it seems to me, and responsible for their existence.

What I have said is nonetheless true. From time to time I meet people who live among riches I cannot even imagine. I still have to make an effort to realize that others can feel envious of such wealth. A long time ago, I once lived a whole week luxuriating in all the goods of this world: we slept without a roof, on a beach, I lived on fruit, and spent half my days alone in the water. I learned something then that has always made me react to the signs of comfort or of a well-appointed house with irony, impatience, and sometimes anger. Although I live without worrying about tomorrow now, and therefore count myself among the privileged, I don't know how to own things. What I do have, which always comes to me without my asking for it, I can't seem to keep. Less from extravagance, I think, than from another kind of parsimony: I cling like a miser to the freedom that disappears as soon as there is an excess of things. For me, the greatest luxury has always coincided with a certain bareness. I love the bare interiors of Spanish or North African houses. Where I prefer to live and work (and what is more unusual, where I would not mind dying) is in a hotel room. I have never been able to succumb to what is called home life (so often the very opposite of an inner life); "bourgeois" happiness bores and terrifies me. This incapacity is nothing to brag about: it has made no small contribution to my worst faults. I don't envy anyone anything, which is my right, but I am not always mindful of the wants of others and this robs me of imagination, that is to say, kindness. I've invented a maxim for my own personal use: "We must put our principles into great things, mercy is enough for the small ones." Alas! We invent maxims to fill the holes in our own natures. With me, a better word for the aforementioned mercy would be indifference. The results, as one can imagine, are less than miraculous.

But all I want to emphasize is that poverty does not necessarily involve envy. Even later, when a serious illness temporarily deprived me of the natural vigor that always transfigured everything for me, in spite of the invisible infirmities and new weaknesses this illness brought, I may have known fear and discouragement, but never bitterness. The illness surely added new limitations, the hardest ones, to those I had already. In the end it encouraged that freedom of the heart, that slight detachment from human concerns, which has always saved me from resentment. Since living in Paris I have learned this is a royal privilege. I've enjoyed it without restrictions or remorse, and until now at any rate, it has illuminated my whole life. As an artist, for example, I began by admiring others, which in a way is heaven on earth. (The present custom in France, as everyone knows, is to launch and even to conclude one's literary career by choosing an artist to make fun of.) My human passions, like my literary ones, have never been directed *against* others. The people I have loved have always been better and greater than I. Poverty as I knew it taught me not resentment but a certain fidelity and silent tenacity. If I have ever forgotten them, either I or my faults are to blame, not the world I was born into.

The memory of those years has also kept me from ever

feeling satisfied in the exercise of my craft. Here, as simply as I can, I'd like to bring up something writers normally never mention. I won't even allude to the satisfaction one supposedly feels at a perfectly written book or page. I don't know whether many writers experience it. As far as I'm concerned, I don't think I've ever found delight in re-reading a finished page. I will even admit, ready to be taken at my word, that the success of some of my books has always surprised me. Of course, rather shabbily, one gets used to it. Even today, though, I feel like an apprentice compared to certain living writers I rank at their true worth. One of the foremost is the man to whom these essays were dedicated as long as twenty years ago. Naturally, a writer has some joys he lives for and that do satisfy him fully. But for me, these come at the moment of conception, at the instant when the subject reveals itself, when the articulation of the work sketches itself out before the suddenly heightened awareness, at those delicious moments when imagination and intelligence are fused. These moments disappear as they are born. What is left is the execution, that is to say, a long period of hard work.

On another level, an artist also has the delights of vanity. The writer's profession, particularly in French society, is largely one of vanity. I say this without scorn, and with only slight regret. In this respect I am like everyone else; who is impervious to this ridiculous disease? Yet, in a society where envy and derision are the rule, the day comes when, covered with scorn, writers pay dearly for these poor joys. Actually, in twenty years of literary life, my work has brought very few such joys, fewer and fewer as time has passed.

Isn't it the memory of the truths glimpsed in *The Wrong Side and the Right Side* that has always kept me from feeling at ease in the public exercise of my craft and has prompted the many refusals that have not always won me friends? By ignoring compliments and homages we lead the person paying those compliments to think we look down on him, when in fact we are only doubting ourselves. By the same token, if I had shown the mixture of harshness and indulgence sometimes found in literary careers, if like so many others I had exaggerated a bit, I might have been looked upon more favorably, for I would have been playing the game. But what's to be done, the game does not amuse me! The ambitions of a Lucien de Rubempré or a Julien Sorel often disconcert me in their naïveté and their modesty. Nietzsche's, Tolstoy's, or Melville's overwhelm me, precisely because of their failure. I feel humility, in my heart of hearts, only in the presence of the poorest lives or the greatest adventures of the mind. Between the two is a society I find ludicrous.

Sometimes on those opening nights at the theater, which are the only times I ever meet what is insolently referred to as "*le Tout-Paris*," it seems to me that the audience is about to vanish, that this fashionable world does not exist. It is the others who seem real to me, the tall figures sounding forth upon the stage. Resisting the impulse to flee, I make myself remember that everyone in the audience also has a rendezvous with himself: that he knows it and will doubtless be keeping it soon. Immediately he seems like a brother once more; solitudes unite those society separates. Knowing this, how can one flatter this world, seek its petty privileges, agree to congratulate every author of every book, and openly thank the favorable critic. Why try to seduce the enemy, and above all how is one to receive the compliments and admiration that the French (in the author's presence anyway, for once he leaves the room! . . .) dispense as generously as Pernod or the fan magazines. I can't do it and that's a fact. Perhaps there is a lot of that churlish pride of mine here, whose strength and extent I know only too well. But if this were all, if only my vanity were involved, it seems to me that I ought to enjoy compliments, superficially at least, instead of repeatedly being embarrassed by them. No, the vanity I share with others comes mostly when I react to criticisms that have some measure of truth. It's not conceit that makes me greet compliments with that stupid, ungrateful look I know so well, but (along with the profound indifference that haunts me like a natural infirmity) a strange feeling that comes over me: "You're missing the point . . ." Yes, they are missing the point, and that is why a reputation, as it's called, is sometimes so hard to bear that one takes a kind of malicious pleasure in doing everything one can to lose it. On the other hand, re-reading *The Wrong Side and the Right Side* for this edition after so many years, I know instinctively that certain pages, despite their inadequacies, *are* the point. I mean that old woman, a silent mother, poverty, light on the Italian olive trees, the populated loneliness of love—all that in my opinion reveals the truth.

Since these pages were written, I have grown older and lived through many things. I have learned to recognize my limits and nearly all my weaknesses. I've learned less about people, since their destiny interests me more than their reactions, and destinies tend to repeat each other. I've learned at least that other people do exist, and that selfishness, although it cannot be denied, must try to be clear-sighted. To enjoy only oneself is impossible, I know, although I have great gifts in this direction. If solitude exists, and I don't know if it does, one should certainly have the right to dream of it occasionally as paradise. I do from time to time, like everyone else. Yet two tranquil angels have always kept me from that paradise: one has a friend's face, the other an enemy's. Yes, I know all this and I've also learned or nearly learned the price of love. But about life itself I know no more than what is said so clumsily in *The Wrong Side and the Right Side*.

"There is no love of life without despair of life," I wrote, rather pompously, in these pages. I didn't know at the time how right I was; I had not yet been through years of real despair. They came, and managed to destroy everything in me except an uncontrolled appetite for life. I still suffer from this both fruitful and destructive passion that bursts through even the gloomiest pages of *The Wrong Side and the Right Side*. It's been said we really *live* for only a few hours of our life. This is true in one sense, false in another. For the hungry ardor one can sense in these essays has never left me; in the last analysis, this appetite is life at its best and at its worst. I've certainly tried to correct its worst effects. Like everyone, I've done my best to improve my nature by means of ethics. Alas, the price has been high. With energy, something I've a good deal of, one sometimes manages to behave morally, but never to *be* moral. To long for morality when one is a man of passion is to yield to *injustice* at the very moment one speaks of justice. Man sometimes seems to me a walking injustice: I am thinking of myself. If I now have the impression I was wrong, or that I lied sometimes in what I wrote, it is because I do not know how to treat my iniquity honestly. Surely I've never claimed to be a just man. I've only said that we should try to be just, and also that such an ambition involves suffering and unhappiness. But is this distinction so important? And can the man who does not even manage to make justice prevail in his own life preach its virtues to other people? If only we could live according to honor—that virtue of the unjust! But our society finds the word obscene; "aristocratic" is a literary and philosophical insult. I am not an aristocrat, my reply is in this book: here are my people, my teachers, my ancestry, here is what, through them, links me with everyone. And yet I do need honor, because I am not big enough to do without it!

What does it matter? I merely wanted to show that if I have come a long way since this book, I have not made much progress. Often, when I thought I was moving forward, I was losing ground. But, in the end, my needs, my errors, and my fidelities have always brought me back to the ancient path I began to explore in *The Wrong Side and the Right Side*, whose traces are visible in everything I've done since, and along which on certain mornings in Algiers, for example, I still walk with the same slight intoxication.

If this is so, why have I so long refused to produce this feeble testimony? First of all because, I must repeat, I have artistic scruples just as other men have moral and religious ones. If I am stuck with the notion "such things are not done," with taboos in general rather alien to my free nature, it's because I am the slave, and an admiring one, of a severe artistic tradition. Since this uneasiness may be at war with my profound anarchy, it strikes me as useful. I know my disorder, the violence of certain instincts, the graceless abandon into which I can throw myself. In order to be created, a work of art must first of all make use of the dark forces of the soul. But not without channeling them, surrounding them with dikes, so that the water in them rises. Perhaps my dikes are still too high today. From this, the occasional stiffness . . . Someday, when a balance is established between what I am and what I say, perhaps then, and I scarcely dare write it, I shall be able to construct the work I dream of. What I have tried to say here is that in one way or another it will be like *The Wrong Side and the Right Side* and that it will speak of a certain form of love. The second reason I've kept these early essays to myself will then be clear: clumsiness and disorder reveal too much of the secrets closest to our hearts; we also betray them through too careful a disguise. It is better to wait until we are skillful enough to give them a form that does not stifle their voice, until we know how to mingle nature and art in fairly equal doses; in short, to be. For being consists of being able to do everything at the same time. In art, everything comes at once or not at all; there is no light without flame. Stendhal once cried: "But my soul is a fire which suffers if it does not blaze." Those who are like him in this should create only when afire. At the height of the flame, the cry leaps straight upward and creates words which in their turn reverberate. I am talking here about what all of us, artists unsure of being artists, but certain that we are nothing else, wait for day after day, so that in the end we may agree to live.

Why then, since I am concerned with what is probably a vain expectation, should I now agree to republish these essays? First of all because a number of readers have been able to find a convincing argument.* And then, a time always comes in an artist's life when he must take his bearings, draw closer to his own center, and then try to stay there. Such is my position today, and I need say no more about it. If, in spite of so many efforts to create a language and bring myths to life, I never manage to rewrite *The Wrong Side and the Right Side*, I shall have achieved nothing. I feel this in my bones. But nothing prevents me from dreaming that I shall succeed, from imagining that I shall still place at the center of this work the admirable silence of a mother and one man's effort to rediscover a justice or a love to match this silence. In the dream that life is, here is man, who finds his truths and loses them on this mortal earth, in order to return through wars, cries, the folly of justice and love, in short through pain, toward that tranquil land where death itself is a happy silence. Here still ... Yes, nothing prevents one from dreaming, in the very hour of exile, since at least I know this, with sure and certain knowledge: a man's work is nothing but this slow trek to rediscover, through the detours of art, those two or three

---

*A simple one. "This book already exists, but in a small number of copies sold by booksellers at a very high price. Why should wealthy readers be the only ones with the right to read it?" Why indeed?

great and simple images in whose presence his heart first opened. This is why, perhaps, after working and producing for twenty years, I still live with the idea that my work has not even begun. From the moment that the republication of these essays made me go back to the first pages I wrote, it was mainly this I wanted to say.

Irony

Two years ago, I knew an old woman. She was suffering from an illness that had almost killed her. The whole of her right side had been paralyzed. Only half of her was in this world while the other was already foreign to her. This bustling, chattering old lady had been reduced to silence and immobility. Alone day after day, illiterate, not very sensitive, her whole life was reduced to God. She believed in him. The proof is that she had a rosary, a lead statue of Christ, and a stucco statue of Saint Joseph carrying the infant Jesus. She doubted her illness was incurable, but said it was so that people would pay attention to her. For everything else, she relied on the God she loved so poorly.

One day someone did pay attention to her. A young

man. (He thought there was a truth and also knew that this woman was going to die, but did not worry about solving this contradiction.) He had become genuinely interested in the old woman's boredom. She felt it. And his interest was a godsend for the invalid. She was eager to talk about her troubles: she was at the end of her tether, and you have to make way for the rising generation. Did she get bored? Of course she did. No one spoke to her. She had been put in her corner, like a dog. Better to be done with it once and for all. She would sooner die than be a burden to anyone.

Her voice had taken on a quarrelsome note, like someone haggling over a bargain. Still, the young man understood. Nonetheless, he thought being a burden on others was better than dying. Which proved only one thing: that he had surely never been a burden to any one. And of course he told the old lady—since he had seen the rosary: "You still have God." It was true. But even here she had her troubles. If she happened to spend rather a long time in prayer, if her eyes strayed and followed a pattern in the wallpaper, her daughter would say: "There she is, praying again!" "What business is that of yours?" the invalid would say. "It's none of my business, but eventually it gets on my nerves." And the old woman would fall silent, casting a long, reproachful look at her daughter.

The young man listened to all this with an immense, unfamiliar pain that hurt his chest. And the old woman went on: "She'll see when she's old. She'll need it too."

You felt that this old woman had been freed of everything except God, wholly abandoned to this final evil, virtuous through necessity, too easily convinced that what still remained for her was the only thing worth loving, finally and irrevocably plunged into the wretchedness of man in God. But if hope in life is reborn, God is powerless against human interests.

They had sat down at the table. The young man had been invited to dinner. The old lady wasn't eating, because it is difficult to digest in the evening. She had stayed in her corner, sitting behind the young man who had been listening to her. And because he felt he was being watched he couldn't eat very much. Nevertheless, the dinner progressed. They decided to extend the party by going to the cinema. As it happened, there was a funny film on that week. The young man had blithely accepted, without thinking about the person who continued to exist behind his back.

The guests had risen from table to go and wash their hands before leaving. There was obviously no question of the old lady's going too. Even if she hadn't been half-paralyzed, she was too ignorant to be able to understand the film. She said she didn't like the movies. The truth was she couldn't understand them. In any case, she was in her corner, vacantly absorbed in the beads of her rosary. This was where she put all her trust. The three objects she kept near her represented the material point where God began. Beyond and behind the rosary, the statue of Christ, or of Saint Joseph, opened a vast, deep blackness in which she placed all her hope.

Everyone was ready. They went up to the old lady to kiss her and wish her a good night. She had already realized what was happening and was clutching her rosary tightly in her hand. But it was plain this showed as much despair as zeal. Everyone else had kissed her. Only the young man was left. He had given her an affectionate handshake and was already turning away. But she saw that the one person who had taken an interest in her was leaving. She didn't want to be alone. She could already feel the horror of loneliness, the long, sleepless hours, the frustrating intimacy with God. She was afraid, could now rely only on man, and, clinging to the one person who had shown any interest in her, held on to his hand, squeezing it, clumsily thanking him in order to justify this insistence. The young man was embarrassed. The others were already turning round to tell him to hurry up. The movie began at nine and it was better to arrive early so as not to have to wait in line.

He felt confronted by the most atrocious suffering he had ever known: that of a sick old woman left behind by people going to the movies. He wanted to leave and escape, didn't want to know, tried to draw back his hand. For a moment, he felt an intense hatred for the old woman, and almost slapped her hard across the face.

Finally he managed to get away, while the invalid, half rising from her armchair, watched with horror as the last certainty in which she could have found rest faded away. Now there was nothing to protect her. And, defenseless before the idea of death, she did not know exactly what terrified her, but felt that she did not want to be alone. God was of no use to her. All He did was cut her off from people and make her lonely. She did not want to be without people. So she began to cry.

The others were already outside in the street. The young man was gripped with remorse. He looked up at the lighted window, a great dead eye in the silent house. The eye closed. The old woman's daughter told the young man: "She always turns the light off when she's by herself. She likes to sit in the dark."

The old man brought his eyebrows triumphantly together, waggling a sententious forefinger. "When I was a young man," he said, "my father used to give me five francs a week out of his wages as pocket money to last me till the following Saturday. Well, I still managed to save. First of all, when I went to see my fiancée, I walked four miles through the open country to get there and four miles to get back. Just you listen to me now, young men just don't know how to amuse themselves nowadays." There were three young men sitting at a round table with this one old man. He was describing his petty adventures—childish actions overblown, incidents of laziness celebrated as victories. He never paused in his story, and, in a hurry to tell everything before his audience left, mentioned only those portions of his past he thought likely to impress them. Making people listen was his only vice: he refused to notice the irony of the glances and the sudden mockery that greeted him. The young man saw in him the usual old bird for whom everything was marvelous in his day, while he thought himself the respected elder whose experience carries weight. The young don't know that experience is a defeat and that we must lose everything in order to win a little knowledge. He had suffered. He never mentioned it. It's better to seem happy. And if he were wrong about this, he would have been even more mistaken to try to make people sympathize with him. What do an old man's sufferings matter when

life absorbs you completely? He talked on and on, wandering blissfully through the grayness of his mutterings. But
it couldn't last. He needed an ending, and the attention of
his listeners was waning. He wasn't even funny any longer;
he was old. And young men like billiards and cards, which
take their minds off the imbecility of everyday work.

Soon he was alone, despite his efforts and the lies he
told to enliven his story. With no attempt to spare his feelings, the young men had left. Once again he was alone.
No longer to be listened to: that's the terrible thing about
being old. He was condemned to silence and loneliness.
He was being told that he would soon be dead. And an
old man who is going to die is useless, he is even an insidious embarrassment. Let him go. He ought to go. Or, if
not, to shut up is the least he can do. He suffers, because
as soon as he stops talking he realizes that he is old. Yet
he did get up and go, smiling to everyone around him. But
the faces he saw were either indifferent, or convulsed by a
gaiety that he had no right to share. A man was laughing:
"She's old, I don't deny it, but sometimes the best stews are
made in old pots." Another, already more seriously: "Well,
we're not rich but we eat well. Look at my grandson now,
he eats more than his father. His father needs a pound of
bread, he needs two! And you can pile on the sausage and
Camembert. And sometimes when he's finished he says:
'Han, han!' and keeps on eating." The old man moved away.
And with his slow step, the short step of the donkey turning the wheel, he walked through the crowds of men on the
long pavements. He felt ill and did not want to go home.
Usually he was quite happy to get home to his table and the

oil lamp, the plates where his fingers mechanically found their places. He still liked to eat his supper in silence, the old woman on the other side of the table, chewing over each mouthful, with an empty head, eyes fixed and dead. This evening, he would arrive home later. Supper would have been served and gone cold, his wife would be in bed, not worrying about him since she knew that he often came home unexpectedly late. She would say: "He's in the moon again," and that would be that.

Now he was walking along with his gently insistent step. He was old and alone. When a life is reaching its end, old age wells up in waves of nausea. Everything comes down to not being listened to any more. He walks along, turns at the corner of the street, stumbles, and almost falls. I've seen him. It's ridiculous, but what can you do about it? After all, he prefers being in the street, being there rather than at home, where for hours on end fever veils the old woman from him and isolates him in his room. Then, sometimes, the door slowly opens and gapes ajar for a moment. A man comes in. He is wearing a light-colored suit. He sits down facing the old man and the minutes pass while he says nothing. He is motionless, just like the door that stood ajar a moment ago. From time to time he strokes his hair and sighs gently. When he has watched the old man for a long time with the same heavy sadness in his eyes, he leaves, silently. The latch clicks behind him and the old man remains, horrified, with an acid and painful fear in his stomach. Out in the street, however few people he may meet, he is never alone. His fever sings. He walks a little faster: tomorrow everything will be different, tomorrow.

Suddenly he realizes that tomorrow will be the same, and, after tomorrow, all the other days. And he is crushed by this irreparable discovery. It's ideas like this that kill one. Men kill themselves because they cannot stand them—or, if they are young, they turn them into epigrams.

Old, mad, drunk, nobody knows. His will be a worthy end, tear-stained and admirable. He will die looking his best, that is to say, he will suffer. That will be a consolation for him. And besides, where can he go? He will always be old now. Men build on their future old age. They try to give this old age, besieged by hopelessness, an idleness that leaves them with no defense. They want to become foremen so they can retire to a little house in the country. But once they are well on in years, they know very well this is a mistake. They need other men for protection. And as far as he was concerned, he needed to be listened to in order to believe in his life. The streets were darker and emptier now. There were still voices going by. In the strange calm of evening they were becoming more solemn. Behind the hills encircling the town there were still glimmers of daylight. From somewhere out of sight, smoke rose, imposingly, behind the wooded hilltops. It rose slowly in the sky, in tiers, like the branches of a pine tree. The old man closed his eyes. As life carried away the rumblings of the town, and the heavens smiled their foolish, indifferent smile, he was alone, forsaken, naked, already dead.

Need I describe the other side of this fine coin? Doubtless, in a dark and dirty room, the old woman was laying the table. When dinner was ready she sat down, looked at the clock, waited a little longer, and then began to eat a hearty meal. She thought to herself: "He is in the moon." That would be that.

There were five of them living together: the grandmother, her younger son, her elder daughter, and the daughter's two children. The son was almost dumb; the daughter, an invalid, could think only with difficulty; and of the two children, one was already working for an insurance company while the other was continuing his studies. At seventy, the grandmother still dominated all these people. Above her bed you could see a portrait taken of her five years before, upright in a black dress that was held together at the neck by a medallion, not a wrinkle on her face. With enormous clear, cold eyes, she had a regal posture she relinquished only with increasing age, but which she still sometimes tried to recover when she went out.

It was these clear eyes that held a memory for her grandson which still made him blush. The old woman would wait until there were visitors and would ask then, looking at him severely, "Whom do you like best? Your mother or your grandmother?" The game was even better when the daughter was present. For the child would always reply: "My grandmother," with, in his heart, a great surge of love for his ever silent mother. Then, when the visitors were surprised at this preference, the mother would say: "It's because she's the one who brought him up."

It was also because the old woman thought that love is something you can demand. The knowledge that she herself had been a good mother gave her a kind of rigidity and intolerance. She had never deceived her husband, and had borne him nine children. After his death, she had brought up her family energetically. Leaving their little farm on the outskirts, they had ended up in the old, poor part of the town where they had been living for a long time.

And certainly this woman was not lacking in qualities. But to her grandsons, who were at the age of absolute judgments, she was nothing but a fraud. One of their uncles had told them a significant story: he had gone to pay a visit to his mother-in-law, and from the outside had seen her sitting idly at the window. But she had come to the door with a duster in her hand and had apologized for carrying on working by saying that she had so little free time left after doing her housework. And it must be confessed that this was typical. She fainted very easily after family discussions. She also suffered from painful vomiting caused by a liver complaint. But she showed not the slightest discretion in the practice of her illness. Far from shutting herself away, she would vomit noisily into the kitchen garbage can. And when she came back into the room, pale, her eyes running with tears from the effort, she would remind anyone who begged her to go to bed that she had to get the next meal ready and carry on in running the house: "I do everything here." Or again: "I don't know what would become of you without me."

The children learned to ignore her vomitings, her "attacks" as she called them, as well as her complaints. One day she went to bed and demanded the doctor. They sent for him to humor her. On the first day he diagnosed a slight stomach upset, on the second a cancer of the liver, on the third a serious attack of jaundice. But the younger of the two children insisted on seeing all this as yet another performance, a more sophisticated act, and felt no concern. This woman had bullied him too much for his initial reaction to be pessimistic. And there is a kind of desperate courage in being lucid and refusing to love. But people who play at being ill can succeed: the grandmother carried simulation to the point of death. On her last day, her children around her, she began freeing herself of the fermentations in her intestines. She turned and spoke with simplicity to her grandson: "You see," she said, "I'm farting like a little pig." She died an hour later.

As for her grandson, he now realized that he had not understood a thing that was happening. He could not free himself of the idea that he had just witnessed the last and most monstrous of this woman's performances. And if he asked himself whether he felt any sorrow, he could find none at all. Only on the day of the funeral, because of the general outburst of tears, did he weep, but he was afraid of being insincere and telling lies in the presence of death. It was on a fine winter's day, shot through with sunlight. In the pale blue sky, you could sense the cold all spangled with yellow. The cemetery overlooked the town, and you could see the fine transparent sun setting in the bay quivering with light, like a moist lip.

None of this fits together? How very true! A woman you leave behind to go to the movies, an old man to whom you have stopped listening, a death that redeems nothing,

and then, on the other hand, the whole radiance of the
world. What difference does it make if you accept everything? Here are three destinies, different and yet alike.
Death for us all, but his own death to each. After all, the
sun still warms our bones for us.

Between Yes and No

If it is true that the only paradises are those we have lost, I know what name to give the tender and inhuman something that dwells in me today. An emigrant returns to his country. And I remember. The irony and tension fade away, and I am home once more. I don't want to ruminate on happiness. It is much simpler and much easier than that. For what has remained untouched in these hours I retrieve from the depths of forgetfulness is the memory of a pure emotion, a moment suspended in eternity. Only this memory is true in me, and I always discover it too late. We love the gentleness of certain gestures, the way a tree fits into a landscape. And we have only one detail with which to re-create all this love, but it will do: the smell of a room too long shut up, the special sound of a footstep on the road. This is the way it is for me. And if I loved then in giving myself, I finally became myself, since only love restores us.

Slow, peaceful, and grave, these hours return, just as strong, just as moving—there is a kind of vague desire in the dull sky. Each rediscovered gesture reveals me to myself. Someone once said to me: "It's so difficult to live." And I remember the tone of voice. On another occasion, someone murmured: "The worst blunder is still to make people suffer." When everything is over, the thirst for life is gone. Is this what's called happiness? As we skirt along these memories, we clothe everything in the same quiet garb, and death looks like a backdrop whose colors have faded. We turn back into ourselves. We feel our distress and like ourselves the better for it. Yes, perhaps that's what happiness is, the self-pitying awareness of our unhappiness.

It is certainly like that this evening. In this Moorish café, at the far end of the Arab town, I recall not a moment of past happiness but a feeling of strangeness. It is already night. On the walls, canary-yellow lions pursue green-clad sheiks among five-branched palm trees. In a corner of the café, an acetylene lamp gives a flickering light. The real light comes from the fire, at the bottom of a small stove adorned with yellow and green enamel. The flames light up the middle of the room, and I can feel them reflected on my face. I sit facing the doorway and the bay. Crouched in a corner, the café owner seems to be looking at my glass, which stands there empty with a mint leaf at the bottom. There is no one in the main room, noises rise from the town opposite, while further off in the bay lights shine. I hear the

Arab breathe heavily, and his eyes glow in the dusk. Is that the sound of the sea far off? The world sighs toward me in a long rhythm, and brings me the peace and indifference of immortal things. Tall red shadows make the lions on the walls sway with a wavelike motion. The air grows cool. A foghorn sounds at sea. The beams from the lighthouse begin to turn: one green, one red, and one white. And still the world sighs its long sigh. A kind of secret song is born of this indifference. And I am home again. I think of a child living in a poor district. That neighborhood, that house! There were only two floors, and the stairs were unlit. Even now, long years later, he could go back there on the darkest night. He knows that he could climb the stairs without stumbling once. His very body is impregnated with this house. His legs retain the exact height of the steps; his hand, the instinctive, never-conquered horror of the banister. Because of the cockroaches.

On summer evenings, the workingmen sit on their balconies. In his apartment, there was only one tiny window. So they would bring the chairs down, put them in front of the house, and enjoy the evening air. There was the street, the ice-cream vendor next door, the cafés across the way, and the noise of children running from door to door. But above all, through the wide fig trees there was the sky. There is a solitude in poverty, but a solitude that gives everything back its value. At a certain level of wealth, the heavens themselves and the star-filled night are nature's riches. But seen from the very bottom of the ladder, the sky recovers its full meaning: a priceless grace. Summer nights mysterious with crackling stars! Behind the child was a stinking corridor, and his little chair, splitting across the bottom, sank a little beneath his weight. But, eyes raised, he drank in the pure night. Sometimes a large tram would rattle swiftly past. A drunk would stand singing at a street corner, without disturbing the silence.

The child's mother sat as silently. Sometimes, people would ask her: "What are you thinking about?" And she would answer: "Nothing." And it was quite true. Everything was there, so she thought about nothing. Her life, her interests, her children were simply there, with a presence too natural to be felt. She was frail, had difficulty in thinking. She had a harsh and domineering mother who sacrificed everything to a touchy animal pride and had long held sway over her weak-minded daughter. Emancipated by her marriage, the daughter came home obediently when her husband died. He died a soldier's death, as they say. One could see his gold-framed military medal and *croix de guerre* in a place of honor. The hospital sent the widow the small shell splinter found in his body. She kept it. Her grief has long since disappeared. She has forgotten her husband, but still speaks of her children's father. To support these children, she goes out to work and gives her wages to her mother, who brings them up with a whip. When she hits them too hard, the daughter tells her: "Don't hit them on the head." Because they are her children she is very fond of them. She loves them with a hidden and impartial love. Sometimes, on those evenings he's remembering, she would come back from her exhausting work (as a cleaning woman) to find the house empty, the old woman out shopping, the children still at school. She would huddle in a chair, gazing in front of her, wandering off in the dizzy pursuit of a crack along the floor. As the night thickened around her, her muteness would seem irredeemably desolate. If the child came in, he would see her thin shape and bony shoulders, and stop, afraid. He is beginning to feel a lot of things. He is scarcely aware of his own existence, but this animal silence makes him want to cry with pain. He feels sorry for his mother; is this the same as loving her? She has never hugged or kissed him, for she wouldn't know how. He stands a long time watching her. Feeling separate from her, he becomes conscious of her suffering. She does not hear him, for she is deaf. In a few moments, the old woman will come back, life will start up again: the round light cast by the kerosene lamp, the oilcloth on the table, the shouting, the swearing. Meanwhile, the silence marks a pause, an immensely long moment. Vaguely aware of this, the child thinks the surge of feeling in him is love for his mother. And it must be, because after all she is his mother.

She is thinking of nothing. Outside, the light, the noises; here, silence in the night. The child will grow, will learn. They are bringing him up and will ask him to be grateful, as if they were sparing him pain. His mother will always have these silences. He will suffer as he grows. To be a man is what counts. His grandmother will die, then his mother, then he.

His mother has given a sudden start. Something has frightened her. He looks stupid standing there gazing at her. He ought to go and do his homework. The child has done his homework. Today he is in a sordid café. Now he is a man. Isn't that what counts? Surely not, since doing homework and accepting manhood leads to nothing but old age.

Still crouching in his corner, the Arab sits with his hands clasped round his feet. The scent of roasting coffee rises from the terraces and mingles with the excited chatter of young voices. The hooting of a tugboat adds its grave and tender note. The world is ending here as it does each day, and all its measureless torments now give rise to nothing but this promise of peace. The indifference of this strange mother! Only the immense solitude of the world can be the measure of it. One evening, they had called her son—he was already quite grown up—to his mother's side. A fright had brought on a serious mental shock. She was in the habit of going out on the balcony at the end of the day. She would take a chair and lean her mouth against the cold and salty iron of the railing. Then she would watch the people going past. Behind her, the night would gradually thicken. In front of her, the shops would suddenly light up. The street would fill with people and lights. She would gaze emptily out until she forgot where she was. On this particular evening, a man had loomed up behind her, dragged her backward, knocked her about, and run away when he heard a noise. She had seen nothing, and fainted. She was in bed when her son arrived. He decided, on the doctor's advice, to spend the night with her. He stretched out on the bed, by her side, lying on the top of the blankets. It was summer. The fear left by the recent drama hung in the air of the overheated room. Footsteps were rustling and doors creaked. The smell of the vinegar used to cool his mother's brow floated in the heavy air. She moved restlessly about, whimpering, sometimes giving a sudden start, which would shake him from his brief snatches of sleep. He would wake drenched in sweat, ready to act—only to fall back heavily after glancing at his watch on which the night fight threw dancing shadows. It was only later that he realized how much they had been alone that night. Alone against the others. The "others" were asleep, while they both breathed the same fever. Everything in the old house seemed empty. With the last midnight trams all human hope seemed drained away, all the certainties of city noises gone. The house was still humming with their passage; then little by little everything died away. All that remained was a great garden of silence interrupted now and then by the sick woman's frightened moans. He had never felt so lost. The world had melted away, taking with it the illusion that life begins again each morning. Nothing was left, his studies, ambitions, things he might choose in a restaurant, favorite colors. Nothing but the sickness and death he felt surrounded by . . . And yet, at the very moment that the world was crumbling, he was alive. Finally he fell asleep, but not without taking with him the tender and despairing image of two people's loneliness together. Later, much later, he would remember this mingled scent of sweat and vinegar, this moment when he had felt the ties attaching him to his mother. As if she were the immense pity he felt spread out around him, made flesh, diligently, without pretense, playing the part of a poor old woman whose fate moves men to tears.

Now the ashes in the grate are beginning to choke the fire. And still the same sigh from the earth. The perfect song of a *derbouka* is heard in the air, a woman's laughter above it. In the bay, the lights come closer—fishing vessels no doubt, returning to harbor. The triangle of sky I see from where I am sitting is stripped of its daylight clouds. Choked with stars, it quivers on a pure breeze and the padded wings of night beat slowly around me. How far will it go, this night in which I cease to belong to myself? There is a dangerous virtue in the word simplicity. And tonight I can understand a man wanting to die because nothing matters anymore when one sees through life completely. A man suffers and endures misfortune after misfortune. He bears them, settles into his destiny. People think well of him. And then, one evening, he meets a friend he has been very fond of, who speaks to him absent-mindedly. Returning home, the man kills himself. Afterwards, there is talk of private sorrows and secret dramas. No, if a reason really must be found, he killed himself because a friend spoke to him carelessly. In the same way, every time it seems to me that I've grasped the deep meaning of the world, it is its simplicity that always overwhelms me. My mother, that evening, and its strange indifference. On another occasion, I was living in a villa in the suburbs, alone with a dog, a couple of cats and their kittens, all black. The mother cat could not feed them. One by one, all the kittens died. They filled the room with their filth. Every evening, when I arrived home, I would find one lying stiff, its gums laid bare. One evening, I found the last one, half eaten by the mother. It stank already. The stench of death mingled with the stench of urine. Then, with my hands in the filth and the stench of rotting flesh reeking in my nostrils, I sat down in the midst of all this misery and gazed for hour after hour at the demented glow in the cat's green eyes as it crouched motionless in the corner. Yes. And it is just like that this evening. When we are stripped down to a certain point, nothing leads anywhere any more, hope and despair are equally groundless, and the whole of life can be summed up in an image. But why stop there? Simple, everything is simple, the lights alternating in the lighthouse, one green, one red, one white; the cool of the night; and the smell of the town and the poverty that reach me from below. If, this evening, the image of a certain childhood comes back to me, how can I keep from welcoming the lesson of love and poverty it offers? Since this hour is like a pause between yes and no, I leave hope or disgust with life for another time. Yes, only to capture the transparency and simplicity of paradises lost—in an image. And so it was not long ago, in a house in an old part of town, when a son went to see his mother. They sat down facing each other, in silence. But their eyes met:

"Well, mother."

"Well, here we are."

"Are you bored? I don't talk much."

"Oh, you've never talked much."

And though her lips do not move her face lights up in a beautiful smile. It's true, he never talked much to her. But did he ever need to? When one keeps quiet, the situation becomes clear. He is her son, she is his mother. She can say to him: "You know."

She is sitting at the foot of the divan, her feet together, her hands together in her lap. He, on his chair, scarcely looks at her and smokes ceaselessly. A silence.

"You shouldn't smoke so much."

"I know."

The whole feeling of the neighborhood rises through the window: the accordion from the café next door, the traffic hurrying in the evening, the smell of the skewers of grilled meat eaten between small, springy rolls of bread, a child crying in the road. The mother rises and picks up her knitting. Her fingers are clumsy, twisted with arthritis. She works slowly, taking up the same stitch three or four times or undoing a whole row with a dull ripping sound.

"It's a little cardigan. I'll wear it with a white collar. With this and my black coat, I'll be dressed for the season."

She has risen to turn on the light.

"It gets dark early these days."

It was true. Summer was over and autumn had not yet begun. Swifts were still calling in the gentle sky.

"Will you come back soon?"

"But I haven't left yet. Why do you mention that?"

"Oh, it was just to say something."

A trolley goes by. A car.

"Is it true I look like my father?"

"The spitting image. Of course, you didn't know him. You were six months old when he died. But if you had a little moustache!"

He mentioned his father without conviction. No memory, no emotion. Probably he was very ordinary. Besides, he had been very keen to go to war. His head was split open in the battle of the Marne. Blinded, it took him a week to die; his name is listed on the local war memorial.

"When you think about it," she says, "it was better that way. He would have come back blind or crazy. So, the poor man . . ."

"That's right."

What is it then that keeps him in this room, except the certainty that it's still the best thing to do, the feeling that the whole *absurd* simplicity of the world has sought refuge here.

"Will you be back again?" she says. "I know you have work to do. Just from time to time . . ."

But where am I now? And how can I separate this deserted café from that room in my past? I don't know any longer whether I'm living or remembering. The beams from the lighthouse are here. And the Arab stands in front of me telling me that he is going to close. I have to leave. I no longer want to make such dangerous descents. It is true, as I take a last look at the bay and its light, that what wells up in me is not the hope of better days but a serene and primitive indifference to everything and to myself. But I must break this too limp and easy curve. I need my lucidity. Yes, everything is simple. It's men who complicate things. Don't let them tell us any stories. Don't let them say about the man condemned to death: "He is going to pay his debt to society," but: "They're going to chop his head off." It may seem like nothing. But it does make a little difference. There are some people who prefer to look their destiny straight in the eye.

Death in the Soul

I arrived in Prague at six in the evening. Right away, I took my bags to the checkroom. I still had two hours to look for a hotel. And I was full of a strange feeling of liberty because I no longer had two suitcases hanging on my arms. I came out of the station, walked by some gardens, and suddenly found myself in the middle of the Avenue Wenceslas, swarming with people at that time of evening. Around me were a million human beings who had been alive all this time whose existence had never concerned me. They were alive. I was thousands of kilometers from home. I could not understand their language. They walked quickly, all of them. And as they overtook and passed me, they cut themselves off from me. I felt lost.

I had little money. Enough to live on for six days. After that, friends would be joining me. Just the same, I began to feel anxious. So I started looking for a cheap hotel. I was in the new part of the town, and all the places I came upon were glittering with lights, laughter, and women. I walked faster. Something in my rapid pace already seemed like flight. Toward eight in the evening, exhausted, I reached the old town. Drawn by a modest-looking hotel with a small doorway, I enter. I fill in the form, take my key. I have room number 34, on the third floor. I open the door to find myself in a most luxurious room. I look to see how much it costs: twice as expensive as I'd thought. The money question is suddenly acute. Now I can live only scrimpingly in this great city. My distress, still rather vague a few moments ago, fixes itself on this one point. I feel uneasy, hollow and empty. Nevertheless, a moment of lucidity: I have always been credited, rightly or wrongly, with the greatest indifference to money. Why should I be worried? But already my mind is working. I must get something to eat, I start walking again and look for a cheap restaurant. I should spend no more than ten crowns on each meal. Of all the restaurants I see, the least expensive is also the least attractive. I walk up and down in front of it. The people inside begin to notice my antics: I have to go in. It is a rather murky cellar, painted with pretentious frescoes. The clientele is fairly mixed. A few prostitutes, in one corner, are smoking and talking seriously to one another. A number of men, for the most part colorless and of indeterminate age, sit eating at the tables. The waiter, a colossus in a greasy dinner jacket, leans his enormous, expressionless head in my direction. I quickly make a random choice of a dish from what, for me, is an incomprehensible menu. But it seems there is need for explanations. The waiter asks a question in Czech. I reply with what little German I know. He does not know German. I'm at a loss. He summons one of the girls, who comes forward in the classic pose, left hand on hip, cigarette in the right, smiling moistly. She sits down at my table and asks questions in a German I judge as bad as my own. Everything becomes clear. The waiter was pushing the *plat du jour*. Game for anything, I order it. The girl talks to me but I can't understand her anymore. Naturally, I say yes in my most sincere tone of voice. But I am not with it. Everything annoys me, I hesitate, I don't feel hungry. I feel a twinge of pain and a tightness in my stomach. I buy the girl a glass of beer because I know my manners. The *plat du jour* having arrived, I start to eat: a mixture of porridge and meat, ruined by an unbelievable amount of cumin. But I think about something else, or rather of nothing at all, staring at the fat, laughing mouth of the woman in front of me. Does she think I am inviting her favors? She is already close to me, starts to make advances. An automatic gesture from me holds her back. (She was ugly. I have often thought that if she had been pretty I would have avoided everything that happened later.) I was afraid of being sick, then and there, in the midst of all those people ready to laugh; still more afraid of being alone in my hotel room, without money or enthusiasm, reduced to myself and my miserable thoughts. Even today, I still wonder with embarrassment how the weary, cowardly creature I then became could have emerged from me. I left. I walked about in the old town, but unable to stomach my own company any longer, I ran all the way to my hotel, went to bed, and waited for sleep, which came almost at once. Any country where I am not bored is a country that teaches me nothing. That was the kind of remark I tried out to cheer myself up. Need I describe the days that followed? I went back to my restaurant. Morning and evening, I endured that atrocious, sickening cumin-flavored food. As a result, I walked around all day with a constant desire to vomit. I resisted the impulse, knowing one must be fed. Besides, what did this matter compared to what I would have had to endure if I had tried a new restaurant? Here, at least, I was "recognized." People gave me a smile even if they didn't speak to me. On the other hand, anguish was gaining ground. I paid too much attention to that sharp twinge of pain in my head. I decided to organize my days, to cover them with points of reference. I stayed in bed as late as possible and the days were consequently shorter. I washed, shaved, and methodically explored the town. I lost myself in the sumptuous baroque churches, looking for a homeland in them, emerging emptier and more depressed after a disappointing confrontation with myself. I wandered along the Vltava and saw the water swirling and foaming at its dams. I spent endless hours in the immense, silent, and empty Hradschin district. At sunset, in the shadow of its cathedral and palaces, my lonely footsteps echoed in the streets. Hearing them, the panic seized me again. I had dinner early and went to bed at half past eight. The sun pulled me out of myself. I visited churches, palaces and museums, tried to soften my distress in every work of art.

A classic dodge: I wanted my rebellion to melt into melancholy. But in vain. As soon as I came out, I was a stranger again. Once, however, in a baroque cloister at the far end of the town, the softness of the hour, the bells tinkling slowly, the clusters of pigeons flying from the old tower, and something like a scent of herbs and nothingness gave rise within me to a tear-filled silence that almost delivered me. Back at the hotel that evening, I wrote the following passage in one sitting: I reproduce it here unchanged, since its very pomposity reminds me of how complex my feelings were: "What other profit can one seek to draw from travel? Here I am, stripped bare, in a town where the signs are strange, unfamiliar hieroglyphics, with no friends to talk to, in short, without any distraction. I know very well that nothing will deliver me from this room filled with the noises of a foreign town, to lead me to the more tender glow of a fireside or a place I'm fond of. Should I shout for help? Unfamiliar faces would appear. Churches, gold, incense, everything flings me back into this daily life where everything takes its color from my anguish. The curtain of habits, the comfortable loom of words and gestures in which the heart drowses, slowly rises, finally to reveal anxiety's pallid visage. Man is face to face with himself: I defy him to be happy ... And yet this is how travel enlightens him. A great discord occurs between him and the things he sees. The music of the world finds its way more easily into this heart grown less secure. Finally stripped bare, the slightest solitary tree becomes the most tender and fragile of images. Works of art and women's smiles, races of men at home in their land and monuments that summarize the centuries, this is the moving and palpable landscape that travel consists of. Then, at twilight, this hotel room where once again the hollow feeling eats at me, as if my soul were hungry." Need I confess that all this was just a means of getting to sleep? I can admit it now. What I remember of Prague is the smell of cucumbers soaked in vinegar that you buy at any street corner to eat between your fingers. Their bitter, piquant scent would awaken my anguish and quicken it as soon as I crossed the threshold of my hotel. That, and perhaps a certain tune played on an accordion as well. Beneath my windows, a blind, one-armed man would sit on his instrument, holding it in place with one buttock while opening and shutting it with his good hand. It was always the same childish, tender tune that woke me every morning, abruptly returning me to the unadorned reality in which I was floundering.

I remember too that on the banks of the Vltava I would suddenly stop, and seized by the scent or the melody, carried almost beyond myself, would murmur: "What does it mean? What does it mean?" But I had doubtless not yet gone over the edge. On the fourth day, at about ten in the morning, I was getting ready to go out. I wanted to see a certain Jewish cemetery I'd not been able to find the day before. Someone knocked at the door of the next room. After a moment's silence, they knocked again. A long knock this time, but apparently there was no answer. A heavy step went down the stairs. Without paying attention to what I was doing, my mind empty, I wasted a few moments reading the instructions for a shaving cream that I had already been using for a month. The day was heavy. A coppery light fell from the gray sky on the spires and domes of old Prague. As they did every morning, the newsboys were calling the name of a newspaper, *Narodni Politika*. I tore myself with difficulty from the torpor that was overcoming me. But just as I was going out, I passed the bellman who looked after my particular floor, armed with a bunch of keys. I stopped. He knocked again, for a long time. He tried to open the door. No success. It must have been bolted on the inside. More knocks. The room sounded so ominously empty that, depressed as I was, I left without asking any questions. But out in the Prague streets a painful foreboding pursued me. How shall I ever forget the bellman's silly face, the funny way his polished shoes curled upward, the button missing from his jacket? I had lunch finally, but with a growing feeling of disgust. At about two in the afternoon, I went back to my hotel.

The staff was whispering in the lobby. I climbed the stairs rapidly, the quicker to face what I was expecting. It was just as I'd thought. The door of the room was half open, so that all that could be seen was a high, blue-painted wall. But the dull light I mentioned earlier threw two shadows on this screen: that of the dead man lying on the bed and a policeman guarding the body. The two shadows were at right angles to each other. The light overwhelmed me. It was authentic, a real light, an afternoon light, signifying life, the sort of light that makes one aware of living. He was dead. Alone in his room. I knew it was not suicide. I dashed back into my room and threw myself on the bed. A man like so many others, short and fat as far as I could tell from his shadow. He had probably been dead for quite a while.

And life had gone on in the hotel, until the bellman had thought of calling him. He had come without suspecting anything and died, alone. Meanwhile, I had been reading the advertisement for my shaving cream. I spent the afternoon in a state that would be hard to describe. I lay on my bed, thinking of nothing, with a strange heaviness in my heart. I cut my nails. I counted the cracks in the floorboards. "If I can count up to a thousand ..." At fifty or sixty, I gave up. I couldn't go on. I could understand nothing of the noises outside. Once, though, in the corridor, a stifled voice, a woman's voice, said in German: "He was so good." Then I thought desperately of home, of my own town on the shores of the Mediterranean, of its gentle summer evenings that I love so much, suffused in green light and filled with young and beautiful women. It was days since I had uttered a single word and my heart was bursting with the cries and protests I had stifled. If anyone had opened his arms to me, I would have wept like a child. Toward the end of the afternoon, broken with weariness, I stared madly at the door handle, endlessly repeating a popular accordion tune in my empty head. At that moment I had gone as far as I could. I had no more country, city, hotel room, or name. Madness or victory, humiliation or inspiration— was I about to *know*, or to be destroyed? There was a knock at the door and my friends came in. I was saved, if disappointed. I believe I even said: "I'm glad to see you again." But I'm sure I stopped there, and that in their eyes I still looked like the man they had left.

I left Prague not long after. And I certainly took an interest in what I saw later. I could note down such and such an hour in the little Gothic cemetery of Bautzen, the brilliant red of its geraniums and the blue morning sky. I could talk about the long, relentless, barren plains of Silesia. I crossed them at daybreak. A heavy flight of birds was passing in the thick, misty morning, above the sticky earth. I also liked Moravia, tender and grave, with its distant, pure horizons, its roads bordered with sour plum trees. But inside I still felt the dizziness of those who have gazed too long into a bottomless pit. I arrived in Vienna, left a week later. Still the numbness held me captive.

Yet in the train taking me from Vienna to Venice, I was waiting for something. I was like a convalescent fed on bouillon wondering how his first crust of bread will taste. Light was about to break through. I know now what it was: I was ready to be happy. I'll mention only the six days I lived on a hill near Vicenza. I am still there, or rather, I still find myself there again occasionally, when the scent of rosemary brings it flooding back.

I enter Italy. A land that fits my soul, whose signs I recognize one by one as I approach. The first houses with their scaly tiles, the first vines flat against a wall made blue by sulphur dressings, the first clothes hung out in the courtyards, the disorder of the men's untidy, casual dress. And the first cypress (so slight and yet so straight), the first olive tree, the dusty fig tree. The soul exhausts its revolts in the shady piazzas of small Italian towns, in noontimes when pigeons look for shelter, in slowness and sloth—passion melts by degrees into tears, and then, Vicenza. Here the days revolve from the daybreak, swollen with roosters' crowing to the unequalled evenings, sweetish and tender, silky behind the cypress trees, their long hours measured by the crickets' chirping. The inner silence that accompanies me rises from the slow pace that leads from each of these days to the next. What more can I long for than this room opening on the plain below, with its antique furniture and its handmade lace. I have the whole sky on my face and I feel as if I could follow these slow, revolving days forever, spinning motionlessly with them. I breathe in the only happiness I can attain—an attentive and friendly awareness. I spend the whole day walking about: from the hill, I go down to Vicenza or else further into the country. Every person I meet, every scent on this street is a pretext for my measureless love. Young women looking after a children's summer camp, the ice-cream vendor's horn (his cart is a gondola on wheels, pushed by two handles), the displays of fruit, red melons with black pips, translucent, sticky grapes— all are props for the person who can no longer be alone.* But the cicadas' tender and bitter chirping, the perfume of water and stars one meets on September nights, the scented paths among the lentisks and the rosebushes, all these are signs of love for the person forced to be alone.† Thus pass the days. After the dazzling glare of hours filled with sun, the evenings come, in the splendid golden backdrop of the sun setting behind the darkness of the cypress trees. I walk along the road toward the crickets one hears from far away. As I advance, one by one they begin to sing more cautiously, and then fall silent. I move forward slowly, oppressed by so much ardent beauty. Behind me, one by

*That is to say, everybody.
†That is to say, everybody.

one, the crickets' voices swell once more: a mystery hangs in this sky from which beauty and indifference descend. In a last gleam of light, I read on the front of a villa: "*In magnificentia naturae, resurgit spiritus.*" This is where I should stop. Already the first star shines, three lights gleam on the hill opposite, night has fallen suddenly, unannounced. A breeze murmurs in the bushes behind me, the day has fled, leaving its sweetness behind.

I had not changed, of course. It was simply that I was no longer alone. In Prague, I was suffocating, surrounded by walls. Here, I was face to face with the world, and liberated from myself. I people the universe with forms in my own likeness. For I have not yet spoken of the sun. Just as it took me a long time to realize my attachment and love for the world of poverty in which I spent my childhood, only now can I see the lesson of the sun and the land I was born in. A little before noon I went out and walked toward a spot I knew that looked out over the immense plain of Vicenza. The sun had almost reached its zenith, the sky was an intense, airy blue. The light it shed poured down the hillsides, clothing cypresses and olive trees, white houses and red roofs in the warmest of robes, then losing itself in the plain that was steaming in the sun. Each time I had the same feeling of being laid bare. The horizontal shadow of that little fat man was still inside me. And what I could touch with my finger in these plains whirling with sunlight and dust, in these close-cropped hills all crusty with burnt grass, was one form, stripped to its essentials, of that taste for nothingness that I carried within me. This country restored my very heart, and put me face to face with my secret anguish. It was and yet was not the anguish I had felt in Prague. How can I explain it? Certainly, looking at this Italian plain, peopled with trees, sunshine, I grasped better than I had before this smell of death and inhumanity that had now been pursuing me for a month. Yes, this fullness without tears, this peace without joy that filled me was simply a very clear awareness of what I did not like—renunciation and disinterest. In the same way, the man who is about to die, and knows it, takes no interest in what will happen to his wife, except in novels. He realizes man's vocation, which is to be selfish—that is to say, someone who despairs. For me, this country held no promise of immortality. What would be the point of feeling alive once more in the soul, if I had no eyes to see Vicenza, no hands to touch the grapes of Vicenza, no skin to feel the night's caress on the road from Monte Berico to the Villa Valmarana?

Yes, all this was true. But the sun filled me also with something else that I cannot really express. At this extreme point of acute awareness everything came together, and my life seemed a solid block to be accepted or rejected. I needed a grandeur. I found it in the confrontation between my deep despair and the secret indifference of one of the most beautiful landscapes in the world. I drew from it the strength to be at one and the same time both courageous and aware. So difficult and paradoxical a thing was enough for me. But perhaps I have exaggerated a bit what I felt then so sincerely. I often think of Prague and the mortal days I spent there. I'm back in my own town again. Occasionally, though, the sour smell of cucumbers and vinegar reawakens my distress. Then I need to think of Vicenza. Both are dear to me, and I find it hard to separate my love of light and life from my secret attachment to the experience of despair that I have tried to describe. It will be clear already that I don't want to bring myself to choose between them. In the suburbs of Algiers, there is a little cemetery with black iron gates. If you go to the far end, you look out over the valley with the sea in the distance. You can spend a long time dreaming before this offering that sighs with the sea. But when you retrace your steps, you find a slab that says "Eternal regrets" on an abandoned grave. Fortunately, there are idealists to tidy things up.

Love of Life

At night in Palma, life recedes slowly toward the tune-filled café district behind the market: the streets are dark and silent until one comes upon latticed doorways where light and music filter through. I spent almost a whole night in one of these cafés. It was a small, very low room, rectangular, painted green and hung with pink garlands. The wooden ceiling was covered with tiny red light bulbs. Miraculously fitted into this minute space were an orchestra, a bar with multicolored bottles, and customers squeezed shoulder to shoulder so tight they could hardly breathe. Just men. In the middle, two square yards of free space. Glasses and bottles streamed by as the waiter carried them to all four corners of the room. No one was completely

sober. Everyone was shouting. Some sort of naval officer
was belching alcohol-laden compliments into my face. An
ageless dwarf at my table was telling me his life story. But
I was too tense to listen. The orchestra was playing tunes
one could only catch the rhythm of, since it was beaten
out by every foot in the place. Sometimes the door would
open. In the midst of shouts, a new arrival would be fitted
in between two chairs.*

Suddenly, the cymbals clashed, and a woman leaped
swiftly into the tiny circle in the middle of the cabaret.
"Twenty-one," the officer told me. I was stupefied. The
face of a young girl, but carved in a mountain of flesh. She
might have been six feet tall. With all her fat she must
have weighed three hundred pounds. Hands on her hips,
wearing a yellow net through which a checkerboard of
white flesh swelled, she was smiling; and each corner of her
mouth sent a series of small ripples of flesh moving toward
her ears. The excitement in the room knew no bounds.
One felt this girl was known, loved, expected. She was still
smiling. She looked around at the customers, still silent
and smiling, and wiggled her belly forward. The crowd
roared, then demanded a song that everyone seemed to
know. It was a nasal Andalusian tune accompanied by a
strong three-beat rhythm from the drums. She sang, and
at each beat mimed the act of love with her whole body.
In this monotonous and passionate movement, real waves
of flesh rose from her hips and moved upward until they
died away on her shoulders. The room seemed stunned.

*There is a certain freedom of enjoyment that defines true civilization. And the
Spanish are among the few peoples in Europe who are civilized.

But pivoting around with the refrain, seizing her breasts with both hands and opening her red, moist mouth, the girl took up the tune in chorus with the audience, until everyone stood upright in the tumult.

As she stood in the center, feet apart, sticky with sweat, hair hanging loose, she lifted her immense torso, which burst forth from its yellow netting. Like an unclean goddess rising from the waves, her eyes hollow, her forehead low and stupid, only a slight quivering at her knees, like a horse's after a race, showed she was still living. In the midst of the foot-stamping joy around her, she was like an ignoble and exalting image of life, with despair in her empty eyes and thick sweat on her belly . . .

Without cafés and newspapers, it would be difficult to travel. A paper printed in our own language, a place to rub shoulders with others in the evenings enable us to imitate the familiar gestures of the man we were at home, who, seen from a distance, seems so much a stranger. For what gives value to travel is fear. It breaks down a kind of inner structure we have. One can no longer cheat—hide behind the hours spent at the office or at the plant (those hours we protest so loudly, which protect us so well from the pain of being alone). I have always wanted to write novels in which my heroes would say: "What would I do without the office?" or again: "My wife has died, but fortunately I have all these orders to fill for tomorrow." Travel robs us of such refuge. Far from our own people, our own language, stripped of all our props, deprived of our masks (one doesn't know the fare on the streetcars, or anything else), we are completely on the surface of ourselves. But also, soul-sick, we

restore to every being and every object its miraculous value.
A woman dancing without a thought in her head, a bottle
on a table, glimpsed behind a curtain: each image becomes
a symbol. The whole of life seems reflected in it, insofar as
it summarizes our own life at the moment. When we are
aware of every gift, the contradictory intoxications we can
enjoy (including that of lucidity) are indescribable. Never
perhaps has any land but the Mediterranean carried me so
far from myself and yet so near.

The emotion I felt at the café in Palma probably came
from this. On the other hand, what struck me in the empty
district near the cathedral, at noon, among the old palaces
with their cool courtyards, in the streets with their scented
shadows, was the idea of a certain "slowness." No one in
the streets. Motionless old women in the miradors. And,
walking along past the houses, stopping in courtyards full
of green plants and round, gray pillars, I melted into this
smell of silence, losing my limits, becoming nothing more
than the sound of my footsteps or the flight of birds whose
shadows I could see on the still sunlit portion of the walls.
I would also spend long hours in the little Gothic cloister
of San Francisco. Its delicate, precious colonnade shone
with the fine, golden yellow of old Spanish monuments. In
the courtyard there were rose laurels, fake pepper plants,
a wrought-iron well from which hung a long, rusty metal
spoon. Passers-by drank from it. I still remember sometimes the clear sound it made as it dropped back on the
stone of the well. Yet it was not the sweetness of life that
this cloister taught me. In the sharp sound of wingbeats
as the pigeons flew away, the sudden, snug silence in the

middle of the garden, in the lonely squeaking of the chain on its well, I found a new and yet familiar flavor. I was lucid and smiling before this unique play of appearances. A single gesture, I felt, would be enough to shatter this crystal in which the world's face was smiling. Something would come undone—the flight of pigeons would die and each would slowly tumble on its outstretched wings. Only my silence and immobility lent plausibility to what looked so like an illusion. I joined in the game. I accepted the appearances without being taken in. A fine, golden sun gently warmed the yellow stones of the cloister. A woman was drawing water from the well. In an hour, a minute, a second, now perhaps, everything might collapse. And yet this miracle continued. The world lived on, modest, ironic, and discreet (like certain gentle and reserved forms of women's friendship). A balance continued, colored, however, by all the apprehension of its own end.

There lay all my love of life: a silent passion for what would perhaps escape me, a bitterness beneath a flame. Each day I would leave this cloister like a man lifted from himself, inscribed for a brief moment in the continuance of the world. And I know why I thought then of the expressionless eyes of Doric Apollos or the stiff, motionless characters in Giotto's paintings.* It was at these moments that I truly understood what countries like this could offer me. I am surprised men can find certainties and rules for life on the shores of the Mediterranean, that they can satisfy their

---

*The decadence of Greek sculpture and the dispersion of Italian art begin with the appearance of smiles and expression in the eyes, as if beauty ended where the mind begins.

reason there and justify optimism and social responsibility. For what struck me then was not a world made to man's measure, but one that closed in upon him. If the language of these countries harmonized with what echoed deeply within me, it was not because it answered my questions but because it made them superfluous. Instead of prayers of thanksgiving rising to my lips, it was this *Nada* whose birth is possible only at the sight of landscapes crushed by the sun. There is no love of life without despair of life.

In Ibiza, I sat every day in the cafés that dot the harbor. Toward five in the evening, the young people would stroll back and forth along the full length of the jetty; this is where marriages and the whole of life are arranged. One cannot help thinking there is a certain grandeur in beginning one's life this way, with the whole world looking on. I would sit down, still dizzy from the day's sun, my head full of white churches and chalky walls, dry fields and shaggy olive trees. I would drink a sweetish syrup, gazing at the curve of the hills in front of me. They sloped gently down to the sea. The evening would grow green. On the largest of the hills, the last breeze turned the sails of a windmill. And, by a natural miracle, everyone lowered his voice. Soon there was nothing but the sky and musical words rising toward it, as if heard from a great distance. There was something fleeting and melancholy in the brief moment of dusk, perceptible not only to one man but also to a whole people. As for me, I longed to love as people long to cry. I felt that every hour I slept now would be an hour stolen from life … that is to say from those hours of undefined desire. I was tense and motionless, as I had been during those vibrant hours at the cabaret in Palma and at the cloister in San Francisco, powerless against this immense desire to hold the world between my hands.

I know that I am wrong, that we cannot give ourselves completely. Otherwise, we could not create. But there are no limits to loving, and what does it matter to me if I hold things badly if I can embrace everything? There are women in Genoa whose smile I loved for a whole morning. I shall never see them again and certainly nothing is simpler. But words will never smother the flame of my regret. I watched the pigeons flying past the little well at the cloister in San Francisco, and forgot my thirst. But a moment always came when I was thirsty again.

The Wrong Side
and the Right Side

She was a lonely and peculiar woman. She kept in close touch with the Spirits, took up their causes, and refused to see certain members of her family who had a bad reputation in this world where she found refuge.

One day, she received a small legacy from her sister. These five thousand francs, coming at the end of her life, turned out to be something of an encumbrance. They had to be invested. If almost everyone is capable of using a large fortune, the difficulty begins when the sum is a small one. The woman remained true to herself. Nearing death, she wanted shelter for her old bones. A real opportunity occurred. A lease had just expired in the local cemetery. On this plot the owners had erected a magnificent, soberly designed black marble tomb, a genuine treasure in fact, which they were prepared to let her have for four thousand francs. She purchased the vault. It was a safe investment, immune to political upheavals or fluctuations in the stock market. She had the inner grave prepared, and kept it in readiness to receive her body. And, when everything was finished, she had her name carved on it in gold letters.

The transaction satisfied her so completely that she was seized with a veritable love for her tomb. At first, she went to see how the work was progressing. She ended up paying herself a visit every Sunday afternoon. It was the only time she went out, and it was her only amusement. Toward two in the afternoon, she made the long trip that brought her to the city gates where the cemetery was. She would go into the little tomb, carefully close the door behind her, and kneel on the *prie-dieu*. It was thus, quite alone with herself, confronting what she was and what she would become, rediscovering the link in a chain still broken, that she effortlessly pierced the secret designs of Providence. A strange symbol even made her realize one day that in the eyes of the world she was dead. On All Saints' Day, arriving later than usual, she found the doorstep of her tomb piously strewn with violets. Some unknown and tender-hearted passers-by, seeing the tomb devoid of flowers, had had the kind thought of sharing their own, and honored her neglected memory.

And now I think about these things again. I can see only the walls of the garden on the other side of my window. And a few branches flowing with light. Higher still, more foliage and, higher still, the sun. But all I can perceive of the air rejoicing outside, of all the joy spread across the world, are the shadows of branches playing on my white curtains. Also five rays of sunlight patiently pouring the scent of dried grass into the room. A breeze, and the shadows on the curtains come to life. If a cloud passes over the sun, the bright yellow of a vase of mimosas leaps from the shadow. This is enough: when a single gleam begins, I'm filled with a confused and whirling joy. It is a January afternoon that puts me this way, face to face with the wrong side of the world. But the cold remains at the bottom of the air. Covering everything a film of sunlight that would crack beneath your finger, but which clothes everything in an eternal smile. Who am I and what can I do but enter into this play of foliage and light? Be this ray of sunlight in which my cigarette burns away, this softness and discreet passion breathing in air. If I try to reach myself, it is at the bottom of this light. And if I try to understand and savor this delicate taste which reveals the secret of the world, it is myself that I find at the depth of the universe. Myself, that is to say, this extreme emotion which frees me from my surroundings.

In a moment—other things, other men, and the graves they purchase. But let me cut this minute from the cloth of time. Others leave a flower between pages, enclosing in them a walk where love has touched them with its wing. I walk too, but am caressed by a god. Life is short, and it is sinful to waste one's time. They say I'm active. But being active is still wasting one's time, if in doing one loses oneself. Today is a resting time, and my heart goes off in search of itself. If an anguish still clutches me, it's when I feel this impalpable moment slip through my fingers like quicksilver. Let those who wish to turn their backs upon the world. I have nothing to complain of, since I can see myself being born. At the moment, my whole kingdom is of this world. This sun and these shadows, this warmth and this cold rising from the depths of the air: why wonder if something is dying or if men suffer, since everything is written on this window where the sun sheds its plenty as a greeting to my pity? I can say and in a moment I shall say that what counts is to be human and simple. No, what counts is to be true, and then everything fits in, humanity and simplicity. When am I truer than when I am the world? My cup brims over before I have time to desire. Eternity is there and I was hoping for it. What I wish for now is no longer happiness but simply awareness.

One man contemplates and another digs his grave: how can we separate them? Men and their absurdity? But here is the smile of the heavens. The light swells and soon it will be summer. But here are the eyes and voices of those I must love. I hold onto the world with every gesture, to men with all my gratitude and pity. I do not want to choose between the right and wrong sides of the world, and I do not like a choice to be made. People don't want one to be lucid and ironic. They say: "It shows you're not nice." I can't see how this follows. Certainly, if I hear someone called an immoralist, my translation is that he needs to give himself an ethic; if I hear of another that he despises intelligence, I realize that he cannot bear his doubts. But this is because I don't like people to cheat. The great courage is still to gaze as squarely at the light as at death. Besides, how can

I define the link that leads from this all-consuming love of life to this secret despair? If I listen to the voice of irony,* crouching underneath things, slowly it reveals itself. Winking its small, clear eye, it says: "Live as if . . ." In spite of much searching, this is all I know.

After all, I am not sure that I am right. But if I think of that woman whose story I heard, this is not what is important. She was going to die, and her daughter dressed her for the tomb while she was alive. Actually, it seems it's easier to do so before the limbs are stiff. Yet it's odd all the same to live among people who are in such a hurry.

*That *guarantee of freedom* Barrès speaks of.

II

Nuptials

1939

(Noces)

The hangman strangled Cardinal Carrafa with a
silken rope that broke: two further attempts were
necessary. The Cardinal looked at the hangman
without deigning to utter a word.
                    —Stendhal, *La Duchesse de Palliano*

Note to the 1950 edition

These essays were originally written in 1936 and 1937, and a small number of copies were published in Algiers in 1938. This new edition reproduces them without any changes, in spite of the fact that their author has not ceased to consider them as essays, in the precise and limited meaning of the term.

Nuptials at Tipasa

In the spring, Tipasa is inhabited by gods and the gods speak in the sun and the scent of absinthe leaves, in the silver armor of the sea, in the raw blue sky, the flower-covered ruins, and the great bubbles of light among the heaps of stone. At certain hours of the day the countryside is black with sunlight. The eyes try in vain to perceive anything but drops of light and colors trembling on the lashes. The thick scent of aromatic plants tears at the throat and suffocates in the vast heat. Far away, I can just make out the black bulk of the Chenoua, rooted in the hills around the village, moving with a slow and heavy rhythm until finally it crouches in the sea.

The village we pass through to get there already opens

on the bay. We enter a blue and yellow world and are welcomed by the pungent, odorous sigh of the Algerian summer earth. Everywhere, pinkish bougainvillaea hangs over villa walls; in the gardens the hibiscus are still pale red, and there is a profusion of tea roses thick as cream, with delicate borders of long, blue iris. All the stones are warm. As we step off the buttercup yellow bus, butchers in their little red trucks are making their morning rounds, calling to the villagers with their horns.

To the left of the port, a dry stone stairway leads to the ruins, through the mastic trees and broom. The path goes by a small lighthouse before plunging into the open country. Already, at the foot of this lighthouse, large red, yellow, and violet plants descend toward the first rocks, sucked at by the sea with a kissing sound. As we stand in the slight breeze, with the sun warming one side of our faces, we watch the light coming down from the sky, the smooth sea and the smile of its glittering teeth. We are spectators for the last time before we enter the kingdom of ruins.

After a few steps, the smell of absinthe seizes one by the throat. The wormwood's gray wool covers the ruins as far as the eye can see. Its oil ferments in the heat, and the whole earth gives off a heady alcohol that makes the sky flicker. We walk toward an encounter with love and desire. We are not seeking lessons or the bitter philosophy one requires of greatness. Everything seems futile here except the sun, our kisses, and the wild scents of the earth. I do not seek solitude. I have often been here with those I loved and read on their features the clear smile the face of love assumes. Here, I leave order and moderation to others. The great free love of nature and the sea absorbs me completely. In this marriage of ruins and springtime, the ruins have become stones again, and losing the polish imposed on them by men, they have reverted to nature. To celebrate the return of her prodigal daughters Nature has laid out a profusion of flowers. The heliotrope pushes its red and white head between the flagstones of the forum, red geraniums spill their blood over what were houses, temples, and public squares. Like the men whom much knowledge brings back to God, many years have brought these ruins back to their mother's house. Today, their past has finally left them, and nothing distracts them from the deep force pulling them back to the center of all that falls.

How many hours have I spent crushing absinthe leaves, caressing ruins, trying to match my breathing with the world's tumultuous sighs! Deep among wild scents and concerts of somnolent insects, I open my eyes and heart to the unbearable grandeur of this heat-soaked sky. It is not so easy to become what one is, to rediscover one's deepest measure. But watching the solid backbone of the Chenoua, my heart would grow calm with a strange certainty. I was learning to breathe, I was fitting into things and fulfilling myself. As I climbed one after another of the hills, each brought a reward, like the temple whose columns measure the course of the sun and from which one can see the whole village, its white and pink walls and green verandas. Like the basilica on the East hill too, which still has its walls and is surrounded by a great circle of uncovered ornamented coffins, most of them scarcely out of the earth, whose nature they still share. They used to contain corpses;

now sage and wallflowers grow in them. The Sainte-Salsa basilica is Christian, but each time we look out through a gap in the walls we are greeted by the song of the world: hillsides planted with pine and cypress trees, or the sea rolling its white horses twenty yards away. The hill on which Sainte-Salsa is built has a flat top and the wind blows more strongly through the portals. Under the morning sun, a great happiness hovers in space.

Those who need myths are indeed poor. Here the gods serve as beds or resting places as the day races across the sky. I describe and say: "This is red, this blue, this green. This is the sea, the mountain, the flowers." Need I mention Dionysus to say that I love to crush mastic bulbs under my nose? Is the old hymn that will later come to me quite spontaneously even addressed to Demeter: "Happy is he alive who has seen these things on earth"? How can we forget the lesson of sight and seeing on this earth? All men had to do at the mysteries of Eleusis was watch. Yet even here, I know that I shall never come close enough to the world. I must be naked and dive into the sea, still scented with the perfumes of the earth, wash them off in the sea, and consummate with my flesh the embrace for which sun and sea, lips to lips, have so long been sighing. I feel the shock of the water, rise up through a thick, cold glue, then dive back with my ears ringing, my nose streaming, and the taste of salt in my mouth. As I swim, my arms shining with water flash into gold in the sunlight, until I fold them in again with a twist of all my muscles; the water streams along my body as my legs take tumultuous possession of the waves—and the horizon disappears. On the beach, I

flop down on the sand, yield to the world, feel the weight
of flesh and bones, again dazed with sunlight, occasionally
glancing at my arms where the water slides off and patches
of salt and soft blond hair appear on my skin.

Here I understand what is meant by glory: the right to
love without limits. There is only one love in this world.
To clasp a woman's body is also to hold in one's arms this
strange joy that descends from sky to sea. In a moment,
when I throw myself down among the absinthe plants to
bring their scent into my body, I shall know, appearances to
the contrary, that I am fulfilling a truth which is the sun's
and which will also be my death's. In a sense, it is indeed my
life that I am staking here, a life that tastes of warm stone,
that is full of the sighs of the sea and the rising song of the
crickets. The breeze is cool and the sky blue. I love this life
with abandon and wish to speak of it boldly: it makes me
proud of my human condition. Yet people have often told
me: there's nothing to be proud of. Yes, there is: this sun,
this sea, my heart leaping with youth, the salt taste of my
body and this vast landscape in which tenderness and glory
merge in blue and yellow. It is to conquer this that I need
my strength and my resources. Everything here leaves me
intact, I surrender nothing of myself, and don no mask:
learning patiently and arduously how to live is enough for
me, well worth all their arts of living.

Shortly before noon, we would come back through the
ruins to a little café by the side of the port. How cool was
the welcome of a tall glass of iced green mint in the shady
room, to heads ringing with colors and the cymbals of the
sun! Outside were the sea and the road burning with dust.

Seated at the table, I would try to blink my eyelids so as
to catch the multicolored dazzle of the white-hot sky. Our
faces damp with sweat, but our bodies cool in light clothing, we would flaunt the happy weariness of a day of nuptials with the world.

The food is bad in this café, but there is plenty of fruit,
especially peaches, whose juice drips down your chin as
you bite into them. Gazing avidly before me, my teeth closing on a peach, I can hear the blood pounding in my ears.
The vast silence of noon hangs over the sea. Every beautiful
thing has a natural pride in its own beauty, and today the
world is allowing its pride to seep from every pore. Why,
in its presence, should I deny the joy of living, as long as
I know everything is not included in this joy? There is no
shame in being happy. But today the fool is king, and I
call those who fear pleasure fools. They've told us so much
about pride: you know, Lucifer's sin. Beware, they used to
cry, you will lose your soul, and your vital powers. I have in
fact learned since that a certain pride . . . But at other times
I cannot prevent myself from asserting the pride in living
that the whole world conspires to give me. At Tipasa, "I see"
equals "I believe," and I am not stubborn enough to deny
what my hands can touch and my lips caress. I don't feel
the need to make it into a work of art, but to describe it,
which is different. Tipasa seems to me like a character one
describes in order to give indirect expression to a certain
view of the world. Like such characters, Tipasa testifies to
something, and does it like a man. Tipasa is the personage
I'm describing today, and it seems to me that the very act
of caressing and describing my delight will ensure that it

has no end. There is a time for living and a time for giving expression to life. There is also a time for creating, which is less natural. For me it is enough to live with my whole body and bear witness with my whole heart. Live Tipasa, manifest its lessons, and the work of art will come later. Herein lies a freedom.

I never spent more than a day at Tipasa. A moment always comes when one has looked too long at a landscape, just as it is a long time before one sees enough of it. Mountains, the sky, the sea are like faces whose barrenness or splendor we discover by looking rather than seeing. But in order to be eloquent every face must be seen anew. One complains of growing tired too quickly, when one ought to be surprised that the world seems new only because we have forgotten it.

Toward evening I would return to a more formal section of the park, set out as a garden, just off the main road. Leaving the tumult of scents and sunlight, in the cool evening air, the mind would grow calm and the body relaxed, savoring the inner silence born of satisfied love. I would sit on a bench, watching the countryside expand with light. I was full. Above me drooped a pomegranate tree, its flower buds closed and ribbed like small tight fists containing every hope of spring. There was rosemary behind me, and I could smell only the scent of its alcohol. The hills were framed with trees, and beyond them stretched a band of sea on which the sky, like a sail becalmed, rested in all its tenderness. I felt a strange joy in my heart, the special joy that stems from a clear conscience. There is a feeling actors have when they know they've played their part well, that is to say, when they have made their own gestures coincide with those of the ideal character they embody, having entered somehow into a prearranged design, bringing it to life with their own heartbeats. That was exactly what I felt: I had played my part well. I had performed my task as a man, and the fact that I had known joy for one entire day seemed to me not an exceptional success but the intense fulfillment of a condition which, in certain circumstances, makes it our duty to be happy. Then we are alone again, but satisfied.

Now the trees were filled with birds. The earth would give a long sigh before sliding into darkness. In a moment, with the first star, night would fall on the theater of the world. The dazzling gods of day would return to their daily death. But other gods would come. And, though they would be darker, their ravaged faces too would come from deep within the earth.

For the moment at least, the waves' endless crashing against the shore came toward me through a space dancing with golden pollen. Sea, landscape, silence, scents of this earth, I would drink my fill of a scent-laden life, sinking my teeth into the world's fruit, golden already, overwhelmed by the feeling of its strong, sweet juice flowing on my lips. No, it was neither I nor the world that counted, but solely the harmony and silence that gave birth to the love between us.

A love I was not foolish enough to claim for myself alone, proudly aware that I shared it with a whole race born in the sun and sea, alive and spirited, drawing greatness from its simplicity, and upright on the beaches, smiling in complicity at the brilliance of its skies.

The Wind at Djemila

There are places where the mind dies so that a truth which is its very denial may be born. When I went to Djemila, there was wind and sun, but that is another story. What must be said first of all is that a heavy, unbroken silence reigned there—something like a perfectly balanced pair of scales. The cry of birds, the soft sound of a three-hole flute, goats trampling, murmurs from the sky were just so many sounds added to the silence and desolation. Now and then a sharp clap, a piercing cry marked the upward flight of a bird huddled among the rocks. Any trail one followed—the pathways through the ruined houses, along wide, paved roads under shining colonnades, across the vast forum between the triumphal arch and the temple set upon a hill—would end at the ravines that surround Djemila on every side, like a pack of cards opening beneath a limitless sky. And one would stand there, absorbed, confronted with stones and silence, as the day moved on and the mountains grew purple surging upward. But the wind blows across the plateau of Djemila. In the great confusion of wind and sun that mixes light into the ruins, in the silence and solitude of this dead city, something is forged that gives man the measure of his identity.

It takes a long time to get to Djemila. It is not a town where you stop and then move further on. It leads nowhere and is a gateway to no other country. It is a place from which travelers return. The dead city lies at the end of a long, winding road whose every turning looks like the last, making it seem all the longer. When its skeleton, yellowish as a forest of bones, at last looms up against the faded colors of the plateau, Djemila seems the symbol of that lesson of love and patience which alone can lead us to the world's beating heart. There it lies, among a few trees and some dried grass, protected by all its mountains and stones from vulgar admiration, from being picturesque, and from the delusions of hope.

We had wandered the whole day in this arid splendor. The wind, which we had scarcely felt at the beginning of the afternoon, seemed to increase as the hours went by, little by little filling the whole countryside. It blew from a gap in the mountains, far to the East, rushing from beyond the horizon, leaping and tumbling among the stones and in the sunlight. It whistled loudly across the ruins, whirled through an amphitheater of stones and earth, bathing the heaps of pock-marked stone, circling each column with its breath and spreading out in endless cries on the forum, open to the heavens. I felt myself whipping in the wind like a mast, hollowed at the waist. Eyes burning, lips cracking, my skin became so dry it no longer seemed mine. Until now, I had been deciphering the world's handwriting on my skin. There, on my body, the world had inscribed the signs of its tenderness or anger, warming with its summer breath or biting with its frosty teeth. But rubbed against for so long by the wind, shaken for more than an hour, staggering from resistance to it, I lost consciousness of the pattern my body traced. Like a pebble polished by the tides, I was polished by the wind, worn through to the very soul. I was a portion of the great force on which I drifted, then much of it, then entirely it, confusing the throbbing of my own heart with the great sonorous beating of this omnipresent natural heart. The wind was fashioning me in the image of the burning nakedness around me. And its fugitive embrace gave me, a stone among stones, the solitude of a column or an olive tree in the summer sky.

The violent bath of sun and wind drained me of all strength. I scarcely felt the quivering of wings inside me, life's complaint, the weak rebellion of the mind. Soon, scattered to the four corners of the earth, self-forgetful and self-forgotten, I am the wind and within it, the columns and the archway, the flagstones warm to the touch, the pale mountains around the deserted city. And never have I felt so deeply and at one and the same time so detached from myself and so present in the world.

Yes, I am present. And what strikes me at this moment

is that I can go no further—like a man sentenced to life imprisonment, to whom everything is present. But also like a man who knows that tomorrow will be the same, and every other day. For when a man becomes conscious of what he is now, it means he expects nothing further. If there are landscapes like moods, they are the most vulgar. All through this country I followed something that belonged not to me but to it, something like a taste for death we both had in common. Between the columns with their now lengthening shadows anxieties dissolved into the air like wounded birds. And in their place came an arid lucidity. Anxiety springs from living hearts. But calm will hide this living heart: this is all I can see clearly. As the day moved forward, as the noises and lights were muffled by the ashes falling from the sky, deserted by myself, I felt defenseless against the slow forces within me that were saying no.

Few people realize that there is a refusal that has nothing to do with renunciation. What meaning do words like future, improvement, good job have here? What is meant by the heart's progress? If I obstinately refuse all the "later on's" of this world, it is because I have no desire to give up my present wealth. I do not want to believe that death is the gateway to another life. For me, it is a closed door. I do not say it is a step we must all take, but that it is a horrible and dirty adventure. Everything I am offered seeks to deliver man from the weight of his own life. But as I watch the great birds flying heavily through the sky at Djemila, it is precisely a certain weight of life that I ask for and obtain. If I am at one with this passive passion, the rest ceases to concern me. I have too much youth in me to be able to speak of death. But it seems to me that if I had to speak of it, I would find the right word here between horror and silence to express the conscious certainty of a death without hope.

We live with a few familiar ideas. Two or three. We polish and transform them according to the societies and the men we happen to meet. It takes ten years to have an idea that is really one's own—that one can talk about. This is a bit discouraging, of course. But we gain from this a certain familiarity with the splendor of the world. Until then, we have seen it face to face. Now we need to step aside to see its profile. A young man looks the world in the face. He has not had time to polish the idea of death or of nothingness, even though he has gazed on their full horror. That is what youth must be like, this harsh confrontation with death, this physical terror of the animal who loves the sun. Whatever people may say, on this score at least, youth has no illusions. It has had neither the time nor the piety to build itself any. And, I don't know why, but faced with this ravined landscape, this solemn and lugubrious cry of stone, Djemila, inhuman at nightfall, faced with this death of colors and hope, I was certain that when they reach the end of their lives, men worthy of the name must rediscover this confrontation, deny the few ideas they had, and recover the innocence and truth that gleamed in the eyes of the Ancients face to face with destiny. They regain their youth, but by embracing death. There is nothing more despicable in this respect than illness. It is a remedy against death. It prepares us for it. It creates an apprenticeship whose first stage is self-pity. It supports man in his great effort to avoid the certainty that he will die completely. But Djemila . . . and then I feel certain that the true, the only, progress of civilization, the one to which a man devotes himself from time to time, lies in creating conscious deaths.

What always amazes me, when we are so swift to elaborate on other subjects, is the poverty of our ideas on death. It is a good thing or a bad thing, I fear it or I summon it (they say). Which also proves that everything simple is beyond us. What is blue, and how do we think "blue"? The same difficulty occurs with death. Death and colors are things we cannot discuss. Nonetheless, the important thing is this man before me, heavy as earth, who prefigures my future. But can I really think about it?

I tell myself: I am going to die, but this means nothing, since I cannot manage to believe it and can only experience other people's death. I have seen people die. Above all, I have seen dogs die. It was touching them that overwhelmed me. Then I think of flowers, smiles, the desire for women, and realize that my whole horror of death lies in my anxiety to live. I am jealous of those who will live and for whom flowers and the desire for women will have their full flesh and blood meaning. I am envious because I love life too much not to be selfish. What does eternity matter to me? You can be lying in bed one day and hear someone say: "You are strong and I owe it to you to be honest: I can tell you that you are going to die"; you're there, with your whole life in your hands, fear in your bowels, looking the fool. What else matters: waves of blood come throbbing to my temples and I feel I could smash everything around me.

But men die in spite of themselves, in spite of their surroundings. They are told: "When you get well . . . ," and they die. I want none of that. For if there are days when nature lies, there are others when she tells the truth. Djemila is telling the truth tonight, and with what sad, insistent beauty! As for me, here in the presence of this world, I have no wish to lie or to be lied to. I want to keep my lucidity to the last, and gaze upon my death with all the fullness of my jealousy and horror. It is to the extent I cut myself off from the world that I fear death most, to the degree I attach myself to the fate of living men instead of contemplating the unchanging sky. Creating conscious deaths is to diminish the distance that separates us from the world and to accept a consummation without joy, alert to rapturous images of a world forever lost. And the melancholy song of the Djemila hills plunges this bitter lesson deeper in my soul.

Toward evening, we were climbing the slopes leading to the village and, retracing our steps, listened to explanations: "Here is the pagan town; this area outside the field is where the Christians lived. Later on . . ." Yes, it is true. Men and societies have succeeded one another in this place; conquerors have marked this country with their noncommissioned officers' civilization. They had a vulgar and ridiculous idea of greatness, measuring the grandeur of their empire by the surface it covered. The miracle is that the ruin of their civilization is the very negation of their ideal. For this skeleton town, seen from high above as evening closes in and white flights of pigeons circle round the triumphal arch, engraved no signs of conquest or ambition on the sky. The world always conquers history in the end. The great shout of stone that Djemila hurls between the mountains, the sky, and the silence—well do I know its poetry: lucidity, indifference, the true signs of beauty or despair. The heart tightens at the grandeur we've already left behind. Djemila remains with its sad watery sky, the song of a bird from the other side of the plateau, the sudden, quick scurrying of goats along the mountainside, and, in the calm, resonant dusk, the living face of a horned god on the pediment of an altar.

Summer in Algiers

to Jacques Heurgon

They are often secret, the love affairs we have with cities. Old towns like Paris, Prague, and even Florence are closed in upon themselves in such a way as to delimit their domain. But Algiers and a few other privileged coastal towns open into the sky like a mouth or a wound. What one can fall in love with in Algiers is what everybody lives with: the sea, visible from every corner, a certain heaviness of the sunlight, the beauty of the people. And, as usual, such generosity and lack of shame emit a more secret perfume. In Paris, one can yearn for space and for the beating of wings. Here, at least, man has everything he needs, and his desires thus assured, can take the measure of his riches.

One probably has to live a long time in Algiers to understand how desiccating an excess of nature's blessings can be. There is nothing here for people seeking knowledge, education, or self-improvement. The land contains no lessons. It neither promises nor reveals anything. It is content to give, but does so profusely. Everything here can be seen with the naked eye, and is known the very moment it is enjoyed. The pleasures have no remedies and their joys remain without hope. What the land needs are clear-sighted souls, that is to say, those without consolation. It asks that we make an act of lucidity as one makes an act of faith. A strange country, which gives the men it nourishes both their splendor and their misery. It is not surprising that the sensual riches this country offers so profusely to the sensitive person should coincide with the most extreme deprivation. There is no truth that does not also carry bitterness. Why then should it be surprising if I never love the face of this country more than in the midst of its poorest inhabitants?

Throughout their youth, men find a life here that matches their beauty. Decline and forgetfulness come later. They have wagered on the flesh, knowing they would lose. In Algiers, to the young and vital everything is a refuge and a pretext for rejoicing: the bay, the sun, games on the red and white terraces overlooking the sea, the flowers and stadiums, the cool-limbed girls. But for the man who has lost his youth there is nothing to hang on to, and no outlet for melancholy. Elsewhere—on Italian terraces, in European cloisters, or in the shape of the hills in Provence—there are places where a man can shed his humanity and gently find salvation from himself. But everything here demands solitude and young blood. On his deathbed, Goethe called for light, and this is a historic remark. In Belcourt and Bab-el-Oued, old men sitting at the back of cafés listen to the young, with brilliantined hair, boasting of their exploits.

It is summer in Algiers that grants us these beginnings and these endings. During the summer months, the town is deserted. But the poor and the sky remain. We go down with them to the harbor and its treasures: the water's gentle warmth and the women's brown bodies. In the evening, swollen with these riches, the people return to oilcloth and kerosene lamp, the meager furniture of their existence.

In Algiers, you don't talk about "going swimming" but about "knocking off a swim." I won't insist. People swim in the harbor and then go rest on the buoys. When you pass a buoy where a pretty girl is sitting, you shout to your friends: "I tell you it's a seagull." These are healthy pleasures. They certainly seem ideal to the young men, since most of them continue this life during the winter, stripping down for a frugal lunch in the sun at noontime every day. Not that they have read the boring sermons of our nudists, those protestants of the body (there is a way of systematizing the body that is as exasperating as systems for the soul). They just "like being in the sun." It would be hard to exaggerate the significance of this custom in our day. For the first time in two thousand years the body has been shown naked on the beaches. For twenty centuries, men have strived to impose decency on the insolence and simplicity of the Greeks, to diminish the flesh and elaborate our dress. Today, reaching back over this history, young men sprinting on the Mediterranean beaches are rediscovering the magnificent motion of the athletes of Delos. Living so close to other bodies, and through one's own body, one finds it has its own nuances, its own life, and, to venture an absurdity, its own psychology.* The evolution of the body, like that of the mind, has its history, its reversals, its gains, and its losses. With only this nuance: color. Swimming in the harbor in the summertime, you notice that everybody's skin changes at the same time from white to gold, then to brown, and at last to a tobacco hue, the final stage the body can attain in its quest for transformation. Overlooking the harbor is a pattern of white cubes, the Casbah. From water level, people's bodies form a bronzed frieze against the glaring white background of the Arab town. And, as one moves into August and the sun grows stronger, the white of the houses grows more blinding and the skins take on a darker glow. How then can one keep from feeling a part of this dialogue between stone and flesh, keeping pace with the sun and the seasons? One spends whole mornings diving to peals of laughter in splashing water, on long canoe trips paddling around the red and black freighters (the Norwegian ones smell of all sorts of wood, the German ones reek of oil, the ones going from port to port along the coast smell of wine and old casks). At the hour when the sun spills from every corner of the sky, an orange canoe laden

---

*May I be foolish enough to say that I don't like the way Gide exalts the body? He asks it to hold back desire in order to make it more intense. This brings him close to those who, in the slang of brothels, are termed "weirdies" or "oddballs." Christianity also seeks to suspend desire. But, more naturally, sees in this a mortification. My friend Vincent, who is a cooper and junior breast-stroke champion, has an even clearer view of things. He drinks when he is thirsty, if he wants a woman he tries to sleep with her, and would marry her if he loved her (this hasn't happened yet). Then he always says: "That feels better!"—an energetic summary of the apology one could write for satiety.

with brown bodies carries us home in one mad sprint. And when, suddenly ceasing the rhythmic stroking of its double fruit-colored wings, we glide into the quiet inner harbor, how can I doubt that what I lead across the silken waters is a cargo of tawny gods, in whom I recognize my brothers?

At the other end of town, summer already offers us the contrast of its other wealth: I mean its silences and boredom. These silences do not always have the same quality, depending on whether they occur in shadow or sunlight. There is a noontime silence on the government square. In the shade of the trees that grow along each side, Arabs sell penny glasses of iced lemonade, perfumed with orange blossom. Their cry of "cool, cool" echoes across the empty square. When it fades away, silence falls again under the sun: ice moves in the merchant's pitcher, and I can hear it tinkling. There is a siesta silence. On the streets around the docks, in front of the squalid barber shops, one can measure it in the melodious buzzing of the flies behind the hollow reed curtains. Elsewhere, in the Moorish cafés of the Casbah, it is bodies that are silent, that cannot drag themselves away, leave the glass of tea, and rediscover time in the beating of their pulse. But, above all, there is the silence of the summer evenings.

These brief moments when day trembles into night must swarm with secret signs and calls to be so closely linked to Algiers in my heart. When I have been away from this country for some time, I think of its twilights as promises of happiness. On the hills looking down over the town, there are paths among the mastic and the olive trees. And it is toward them that my heart turns then. I can see sheaves of black birds rising against the green horizon. In the sky, suddenly emptied of its sun, something releases its hold. A whole flock of tiny red clouds stretches upward until it dissolves into the air. Almost immediately afterward appears the first star, which had been taking shape and growing harder in the thickness of the heavens. And then, sudden and all-enveloping, the night. What is so unique in these fleeting evenings of Algiers that they free so many things in me? They leave a sweetness on my lips that vanishes into the night before I have time to weary of it. Is this the secret of their persistence? The tenderness of this country is overwhelming and furtive. But at least our heart gives way to it completely. The dance hall at Padovani Beach is open every day. And, in this immense rectangular box, open to the sea all along one side, the poor youngsters of the district come to dance until evening. Often, I would wait there for one particular moment. In the daytime, the dance hall is protected by a sloping wooden roof. When the sun has gone down it is removed. The hall fills with a strange green light, born in the double shell of sky and sea. When you sit far from the windows, you can see only the sky, and, like puppets in a shadow theater, the faces of the dancers floating past, one after another. Sometimes they play a waltz, and the dark profiles revolve like cutout figures on a turntable. Night comes quickly and with it the lights. I shall never be able to describe the thrill and the secret enchantment of this subtle moment. I remember a magnificent, tall girl who had danced all one afternoon. She was wearing a necklace of jasmine on her close-fitting blue dress, which was damp with sweat right down the back. She was laughing and throwing back her head as she danced. Passing in front of the tables, she left behind a mingled scent of flowers and flesh. When evening came, I could no longer see her body pressed against her partner, but the white of her jasmine and the black of her hair swirled one after the other against the sky, and when she threw back her breasts I could hear her laugh and see her partner's silhouette lean suddenly forward. I owe my idea of innocence to evenings like these. And I am learning not to separate these beings charged with violence from the sky in which their desires revolve.

At the neighborhood movie houses in Algiers, they sometimes sell pastilles with engraved red mottoes that express everything needed for the birth of love: (A) questions: "When will you marry me?"; "Do you love me?"; (B) replies: "Madly"; "Next spring." After having prepared the ground, you pass them to the girl next to you, who answers in kind or simply plays dumb. At Belcourt, there have been marriages arranged like this, whole lives decided in an exchange of mint candies. And this gives a good picture of the child-like people of this country.

The hallmark of youth, perhaps, is a magnificent vocation for easy pleasures. But, above all, the haste to live borders on extravagance. In Belcourt, as in Bab-el-Oued, people marry young. They start work very early, and exhaust the range of human experience in ten short years. A workingman of thirty has already played all his cards. He waits for the end with his wife and children around him.

His delights have been swift and merciless. So has his life.
And you understand then that he is born in a land where
everything is given to be taken away. In such abundance
and profusion, life follows the curve of the great passions,
sudden, demanding, generous. It is not meant to be built,
but to be burned up. So reflection or self-improvement are
quite irrelevant. The notion of hell, for example, is nothing
more than an amusing joke here. Only the very virtuous
are allowed such fancies. And I even think that virtue is
a meaningless word in Algeria. Not that these men lack
principles. They have their code of morality, which is very
well defined. You "don't let your mother down." You see to it
that your wife is respected in the street. You show consid-
eration to pregnant women. You don't attack an enemy two
to one, because "that's dirty." If anyone fails to observe these
elementary rules "He's not a man," and that's all there is to
it. This seems to me just and strong. There are still many
of us who observe the highway code, the only disinterested
one I know. But at the same time, shopkeeper morality is
unknown. I have always seen the faces around me take on
an expression of pity at the sight of a man between two
policemen. And, before finding out whether the man was a
thief, a parricide, or simply an eccentric, people said: "Poor
fellow," or again, with a touch of admiration: "He's a real
pirate, that one!"

There are people born for pride and for life. It is they
who nourish the most singular vocation for boredom, they
too who find death the most repulsive. Apart from sensual
delights, Algerian amusements are idiotic. A bowling club,
fraternal society dinners, cheap movies, and communal

celebrations have for years now been enough to keep the over-thirty age group entertained. Sundays in Algiers are among the dreariest anywhere. How would these mindless people know how to disguise the deep horror of their lives with myths? In Algiers, everything associated with death is either ridiculous or detestable. The people have neither religion nor idols and die alone after having lived in a crowd. I know no place more hideous than the cemetery on the boulevard Bru, which is opposite one of the most beautiful landscapes in the world. A fearful sadness rises from the accumulated bad taste of its black monuments, revealing death's true face. "Everything passes," the heart-shaped ex-votos read, "but memory." And they all insist on the ridiculous eternity provided at so small a price by the hearts of those who loved us. The same phrases serve all forms of despair. They are addressed to the deceased and speak in the second person singular: "Our memory will never abandon thee"—a gloomy pretense by means of which one lends a body and desires to what is, at best, a black liquid. In another spot, in the midst of a stupefying display of flowers and marble birds, is this reckless vow: "Never shall thy grave lack flowers." But one is quickly reassured: the words are carved around a gilded stucco bouquet, a great timesaver for the living (like those flowers called "everlasting," which owe their pompous name to the gratitude of those who still jump on moving buses). Since one must move with the times, the classical warbler is sometimes replaced by a breath-taking pearly airplane, piloted by a silly-looking angel who, disregarding all logic, has been provided with a magnificent pair of wings.

Still, how can I explain it, these images of death never quite separate themselves from life? The values are closely linked. The favorite joke of Algerian undertakers, driving by in an empty hearse, is to shout "like a ride, honey?" to the pretty girls they meet along the way. There is nothing to keep one from finding this symbolic, if in somewhat bad taste. It may also seem blasphemous to greet the news of someone's death with a wink of the left eye and the comment "Poor guy, he won't sing any more." Or, like the woman from Oran who had never loved her husband: "The Lord gave him to me, the Lord hath taken him away." But when all is said and done, I don't see what is sacred about death, and I am, on the contrary, very aware of the difference between fear and respect. Everything breathes the horror of death in this country that is an invitation to life. And yet it is beneath the walls of this very cemetery that the young men of Belcourt arrange their meetings and the girls let themselves be kissed and fondled.

I fully realize that such people cannot be accepted by everyone. Intelligence does not occupy the place here that it does in Italy. This race is indifferent to the mind. It worships and admires the body. From this comes its strength, its naïve cynicism, and a puerile vanity that leads it to be severely criticized. People commonly reproach its "mentality," that is to say, its particular mode of life and set of values. And it is true that a certain intensity of living involves some injustice. Yet here are a people with no past, with no traditions, though not without poetry. Their poetry has a hard, sensual quality I know very well; it is far from tender, even from the tenderness of the Algerian sky; it is the only poetry, in fact, that moves me and restores me. The opposite of a civilized people is a creative one. These barbarians lounging on the beaches give me the foolish hope that, perhaps without knowing it, they are modeling the face of a culture where man's greatness will finally discover its true visage. These people, wholly engaged in the present, live with neither myths nor consolation. Investing all their assets on this earth, they are left defenseless against death. The gifts of physical beauty have been heaped upon them. And, also the strange greediness that always goes along with wealth that has no future. Everything people do in Algiers reveals a distaste for stability and a lack of regard for the future. People are in a hurry to live, and if an art were to be born here it would conform to the hatred of permanence that led the Dorians to carve their first column out of wood. And still, yes, one can find a certain moderation as well as a constant excess in the strained and violent faces of these people, in this summer sky emptied of tenderness, beneath which all truths can be told and on which no deceitful divinity has traced the signs of hope or of redemption. Between this sky and the faces turned toward it there is nothing on which to hang a mythology, a literature, an ethic, or a religion—only stones, flesh, stars, and those truths the hand can touch.

To feel one's ties to a land, one's love for certain men, to know there is always a place where the heart can find rest—these are already many certainties for one man's life. Doubtless they are not enough. But at certain moments everything yearns for this homeland of the soul. "Yes, it is to this we must return." What is strange about finding on earth the unity Plotinus longed for? Unity expresses itself here in terms of sea and sky. The heart senses it through a certain taste of the flesh that constitutes its bitterness and greatness. I am learning that there is no superhuman happiness, no eternity outside the curve of the days. These ridiculous and essential assets, these relative truths are the only ones that move me. I have not enough soul to understand the other, "ideal" ones. Not that we should behave as beasts, but I can see no point in the happiness of angels. All I know is that this sky will last longer than I shall. And what can I call eternity except what will continue after my death? What I am expressing here is not the creature's complacency about his condition. It is something quite different. It is not always easy to be a man, even less to be a man who is pure. But to be pure means to rediscover that country of the soul where one's kinship with the world can be felt, where the throbbing of one's blood mingles with the violent pulsations of the afternoon sun. It is a well-known fact that we always recognize our homeland at the moment we are about to lose it. Men whose self-torments are too great are those whom their native land rejects. I have no desire to be crude or to seem to exaggerate. But after all what denies me in this life is first of all what kills me. Everything that exalts life at the same time increases its absurdity. In the Algerian summer I learn that only one thing is more tragic than suffering, and that is the life of a happy man. But this can also be the path to a greater life, since it can teach us not to cheat.

Many people, in fact, affect a love of life in order to avoid love itself. They try to enjoy themselves and "to experiment."

But this is an intellectual attitude. It takes a rare vocation to become a sensualist. A man lives out his life without the help of his mind, with its triumphs and defeats, its simultaneous loneliness and companionship. Seeing those men from Belcourt who work, take care of their wives and children, often without a word of complaint, I think that one can feel a certain shame. I certainly have no illusions. There is not much love in the lives I am describing. I should say rather that there is no longer very much. But at least they have eluded nothing. There are some words that I have never really understood, such as sin. Yet I think I know that these men have never sinned against life. For if there is a sin against life, it lies perhaps less in despairing of it than in hoping for another life and evading the implacable grandeur of the one we have. These men have not cheated. They were gods of the summer at twenty in their thirst for life, and they are still gods today, stripped of all hope. I have seen two of them die. They were full of horror, but silent. It is better that way. From the mass of human evils swarming in Pandora's box, the Greeks brought out hope at the very last, as the most terrible of all. I don't know any symbol more moving. For hope, contrary to popular belief, is tantamount to resignation. And to live is not to be resigned.

Such at least is the bitter lesson of summers in Algiers. But already the season trembles and the summer passes. After so much violence and tension, the first September rains are like the first tears of a liberated land, as if for a few days this country were bathed in tenderness. Yet at the same time the carob trees emit the scent of love across

Algeria. In the evening or after the rain, the whole earth lies, its belly moistened with a bitter almond-scented seed, at rest from having yielded all summer long to the sun. And once again this fragrance consecrates the nuptials of man and earth, and gives rise in us to the only truly virile love in this world: one that is generous and will die.

The Desert

to Jean Grenier

Living, of course, is rather the opposite of expressing. If I am to believe the great Tuscan masters, it means bearing triple witness, in silence, fire, and immobility. It takes a long time to realize that one can encounter the faces in these Tuscan paintings any day of the week in the streets of Florence or Pisa. But of course we no longer know how to see the real faces of those around us. We no longer look at our contemporaries, eager only for those points of reference in them that determine our behavior. We prefer its most vulgar poetry to the face itself. As for Giotto and Piero della Francesca, they are perfectly aware that a man's feelings are nothing. Surely everyone has a heart. But the great simple, eternal emotions around which the love of living revolves—hatred, love, tears, and joys—these grow deep inside a man and mold the visage of his destiny, like the grief that makes Mary clench her teeth in Giottino's "Entombment." In the immense friezes of Tuscan churches I make out crowds of angels, their features scarcely traced, but in each mute and passionate face I recognize a solitude.

What matters are not picturesque qualities, episodes, shades of color, or emotional effects. What counts is not poetry. What counts is truth. And I call truth anything that continues. There is a subtle lesson in thinking that, in this respect, only painters can satisfy our hunger. This is because they have the privilege of making themselves novelists of the body. Because they work in that magnificent and trivial matter called the present. And the present always shows itself in a gesture. They do not paint a smile, a fleeting moment of modesty, of regret, or of expectation, but a face with the shape of its bones and the warmth of its blood. What they have expelled from these faces molded for eternity is the curse of the mind: at the price of hope. For the body knows nothing of hope. All it knows is the beating of its own heart. Its eternity consists of indifference. As in the "Scourging of Christ" by Piero della Francesca, where, in a freshly washed courtyard, both the tortured Christ and the thickset executioner reveal the same detachment in their attitudes. This is because the torment has no sequel. Its lesson ends with the frame around the canvas. Why should a man who expects no tomorrow feel emotion? The impassiveness and the greatness that man shows when he has no hope, the eternal present, is precisely what perceptive theologians have called hell. And hell, as everyone knows, also consists of bodily suffering. The Tuscan painters stop at the body and not at its destiny. There are no prophetic paintings. And it is not in museums that we must seek reasons to hope.

The immortality of the soul, it is true, engrosses many noble minds. But this is because they reject the body, the only truth that is given them, before using up its strength. For the body presents no problems, or, at least, they know the only solution it proposes: a truth which must perish and which thus acquires a bitterness and nobility they dare not contemplate directly. Noble minds would rather have poetry than the body, for poetry concerns the soul. Clearly, I am playing on words. But it is also clear that all I wish to do by calling it truth is consecrate a higher poetry: the dark flame that Italian painters from Cimabue to Francesca have raised from the Tuscan landscape as the lucid protestation of men thrown upon an earth whose splendor and light speak ceaselessly to them of a nonexistent God.

Sometimes indifference and insensitivity permit a face to merge with the mineral grandeur of a landscape. Just as certain Spanish peasants come to resemble their own olive trees, so the faces in Giotto's pictures, shorn of the insignificant shadows that reveal the soul, finally merge with Tuscany itself in the only lesson it freely offers: the exercise of passion at the expense of feeling, a mixture of asceticism and pleasure, a resonance common to both man and the earth and by which man, like the earth, defines himself as halfway between wretchedness and love. There are not many truths the heart can be sure of. I realized this one evening as the shadows were beginning to drown the vines and olive trees of the Florentine countryside in a vast and silent sadness. But sadness in this country is never anything but a commentary on beauty. And as the train traveled on through the evening I felt a tension in me slowly relaxing. Can I doubt today that even with the face of sadness, one could call it happiness?

Yes, Italy also lavishes on every landscape the lesson illustrated by its men. But it is easy to miss our chance of happiness, for it is always undeserved. The same is true of Italy. And if its grace is sudden, it is not always immediate. More than any other country, Italy invites us to deepen an experience that paradoxically seems to be complete on first acquaintance. This is because it begins by pouring out its poetry the better to disguise its truth. Italy's first enchantments are rites of forgetfulness: the laurel roses of Monaco, flower-filled Genoa with its smell of fish, and blue evenings on the Ligurian coast. Then finally Pisa, and with it an Italy which has lost the rather tawdry charm of the Riviera. But it is still a land of easy virtue, so why not lend ourselves for a time to its sensual grace? There is nothing urging me on while I am here (I am deprived of the joys of the harried tourist, since a cheap ticket compels me to spend a certain time in the town "of my choice"). My patience for love and understanding seems endless on this first evening when, dead tired and starved, I enter Pisa, greeted on the station platform by ten loudspeakers bellowing out a flood of sentimental songs to an almost entirely youthful crowd. I already know what I expect. After the life here has surged around me, the strange moment will come, when, with the cafés closed and the silence suddenly restored, I'll walk through the short, dark streets toward the center of the town. The black and gold Arno, the green and yellow monuments, the empty town—how can I describe the neat and sudden subterfuge that transforms Pisa at ten each evening into a strange stage-set of silence, water, and stone. "In such a night as this, Jessica!" Here, on this unique stage, gods appear with the voices of Shakespeare's lovers … We must learn how to lend ourselves to dreaming when dreams lend themselves to us. Already I can hear in the depth of this Italian night the strains of the more private song that people come to look for here. Tomorrow, and only tomorrow, the countryside will round out in the morning light. Tonight I am a god among gods, and as Jessica flies off "on the swift steps of love," I mingle my voice with Lorenzo's. But Jessica is only a pretext; this surge of love goes beyond her. Yes, I think Lorenzo is not so much in love with her as grateful to her for allowing him to love. Why should I dream this evening of the lovers of Venice and forget Verona's? Because there is nothing here that invites us to cherish unhappy lovers. Nothing is more vain than to die for love. What we ought to do is live. A living Lorenzo is better than a Romeo in his grave, despite his rosebush. Then why not dance in these celebrations of living love— and sleep in the afternoons on the lawn of the Piazza del Duomo, surrounded by monuments there will always be time enough to visit, drink from the city's fountains where the water is lukewarm but so fluid, and look once more for the face of that laughing woman with the long nose and proud mouth. All we need understand is that this initiation prepares us for higher illuminations. These are the dazzling processions that lead to the Dionysian mysteries at Eleusis. It is in joy that man prepares his lessons and when his ecstasy is at its highest pitch that the flesh becomes conscious and consecrates its communion with a sacred mystery whose symbol is black blood. It is now that the self-forgetfulness drawn from the ardor of that first Italy prepares us for the lesson that frees us from hope and from our history. These twin truths of the body and of the moment, at the spectacle of beauty—how can we not cling to them as to the only happiness we can expect, one that will enchant us but at the same time perish?

The most loathsome materialism is not the kind people usually think of, but the sort that attempts to let dead ideas pass for living realities, diverting into sterile myths the stubborn and lucid attention we give to what we have within us that must forever die. I remember that in Florence, in the cloister of the dead at the Santissima Annunziata, I was carried away by something I mistook for distress, which was only anger. It was raining. I was reading the inscriptions on the tombstones and ex-votos. One man had been a tender father and a faithful husband; another, at the same time the best of husbands and a skillful merchant. A young woman, a model of all the virtues, had spoken French *"si come il nativo."* There was a young girl, who had been the hope of her whole family, *"ma la gioia è pellegrina sulla terra."* None of this affected me. Nearly all of them, according to the inscriptions, had resigned themselves to dying, doubtless because they accepted their other duties. Children had invaded the cloister and were playing leap-frog over the tombstones that strove to perpetuate their virtues. Night was falling, and I had sat down on the ground, my back against a column. A priest smiled at me as he went by. In the church, an organ was playing softly, and the warm color of its pattern sometimes emerged behind the children's shouts. Alone against the column, I was like someone seized by the throat, who shouts out his faith as if it were his last word. Everything in me protested against such a resignation. "You must," said the inscriptions. But no, and my revolt was right. This joy that was moving forward, indifferent and absorbed like a pilgrim treading on the earth, was something that I had to follow step by step. And, as to the rest, I said no. I said no with all my strength. The tombstones were teaching me that it was pointless, that life is *col sol levante, col sol cadente.* But even today I cannot see what my revolt loses by being pointless, and I am well aware of what it gains.

Besides, that is not what I set out to say. I would like to define a little more clearly a truth I felt then at the very heart of my revolt and of which this revolt was only an extension, a truth that stretched from the tiny last roses in the cloister of Santa Maria Novella to the women on that Sunday morning in Florence, their breasts free beneath their light dresses, and their moist lips. On every church corner, that Sunday morning, there were displays of flow-ers, their petals thick and shining, bejeweled with spots of water. I found in them then a kind of "simplicity" as well as a reward. There was a generous opulence in the flowers and in the women, and I could not see that desiring the latter was much different from longing for the former. The same pure heart sufficed for both. It's not often a man feels his heart is pure. But when he does, it is his duty to call what has so singularly purified him truth, even if this truth may seem a blasphemy to others, as is the case with what I thought that day. I had spent the morning in a Franciscan convent, at Fiesole, full of the scent of laurel. I had stood for a long time in a little courtyard overflowing with red flowers, sunlight, and black and yellow bees. In one corner there was a green watering can. Earlier, I had visited the monks' cells, and seen their little tables, each adorned with a skull. Now, the garden testified to their inspiration. I had turned back toward Florence, down the hill that led toward the town lying open with all its cypress trees. I felt this splendor of the world, the women and the flowers, was a kind of justification for these men. I was not sure that they were not also the justification for all men who know that an extreme level of poverty always meets the wealth and luxury of the world. Between the life of these Franciscans enclosed among columns and flowers and the life of the young men of the Padovani beach in Algiers who spend the whole year in the sun, I felt there was a common resonance. If they strip themselves bare, it is for a greater life (and not for another life). At least, that is the only valid meaning of such expressions as "deprivation" and "stripping oneself bare." Being naked always carries a sense of physical liberty and of the harmony between hand and flowers—the loving understanding between the earth and a man delivered

from the human—ah! I would be a convert if this were not
already my religion. No, what I have just said cannot be a
blasphemy—any more than if I say that the inner smile of
Giotto's portraits of Saint Francis justifies those who have
a taste for happiness. For myths are to religion what poetry
is to truth: ridiculous masks laid upon the passion to live.

Shall I go further? The same men at Fiesole who live
among red flowers keep in their cells the skull that nourishes their meditations. Florence at their windows and
death on their tables. A certain continuity in despair can
give birth to joy. And when life reaches a certain tempera-
ture, our soul and our blood mingle and live at ease in contradiction, as indifferent to duty as to faith. I am no longer
surprised that a cheerful hand should thus have summa-
rized its strange notion of honor on a wall in Pisa: *"Alberto
fa l'amore con la mia sorella."* I am no longer surprised that
Italy should be the land of incest, or at least, what is more
significant, of admitted incest. For the path that leads
from beauty to immorality is tortuous but certain. Plunged
deep in beauty, the mind feeds off nothingness. When a
man faces landscapes whose grandeur clutches him by the
throat, each movement of his mind is a scratch on his perfection. And soon, crossed out, scarred and rescarred by so
many overwhelming certainties, man ceases to be anything
at all in the face of the world but a formless stain knowing
only passive truths, the world's color or its sun. Landscapes
as pure as this dry up the soul and their beauty is unbearable. The message of these gospels of stone, sky, and water is
that there are no resurrections. Henceforth, from the depths
of the deserts that the heart sees as magnificent, men of

these countries begin to feel temptation. Why is it surprising if minds brought up before the spectacle of nobility, in the rarefied air of beauty, remain unconvinced that greatness and goodness can live in harmony. An intelligence with no god to crown its glory seeks for a god in what denies it. Borgia, on his arrival in the Vatican, exclaims: "Now that God has given us the papacy, let us hasten to enjoy it." And he behaves accordingly. "Hasten" is indeed the word. There is already a hint of the despair so characteristic of people who have everything.

Perhaps I am mistaken. For I was in fact happy in Florence, like many others before me. But what is happiness except the simple harmony between a man and the life he leads? And what more legitimate harmony can unite a man with life than the dual consciousness of his longing to endure and his awareness of death? At least he learns to count on nothing and to see the present as the only truth given to us "as a bonus." I realize that people talk about Italy, the Mediterranean, as classical countries where everything is on a human scale. But where is this, and where is the road that leads the way? Let me open my eyes to seek my measure and my satisfaction! What I see is Fiesole, Djemila, and ports in the sunlight. The human scale? Silence and dead stones. All the rest belongs to history.

And yet this is not the end. For no one has said that happiness should be forever inseparable from optimism. It is linked to love—which is not the same thing. And I know of times and places where happiness can seem so bitter that we prefer the promise of it. But this is because at such times or places I had not heart enough to love—that is, to persevere in love. What we must talk of here is man's entry into the celebration of beauty and the earth. For now, like the neophyte shedding his last veils, he surrenders to his god the small change of his personality. Yes, there is a higher happiness, where happiness seems trivial. In Florence, I climbed right to the top of the Boboli gardens, to a terrace from which I could see Mount Oliveto and the upper part of the town as far as the horizon. On each of the hills, the olive trees were pale as little wisps of smoke, and the stronger shoots of the cypresses stood out against their light mist, the nearer ones green and the further ones black. Heavy clouds spotted the deep blue of the sky. As the afternoon drew to a close, a silvery light bathed everything in silence. At first the hilltops had been hidden in clouds. But a breeze had risen whose breath I could feel on my cheek. As it blew, the clouds behind the mountains drew apart like two sides of a curtain. At the same time, the cypress trees on the summit seemed to shoot up in a single jet against the sudden blue of the sky. With them, the whole hillside and landscape of stones and olive trees rose slowly back into sight. Other clouds appeared. The curtain closed. And the hill with its cypress trees and houses vanished once more. Then the same breeze, which was closing the thick folds of the curtain over other hills, scarcely visible in the distance, came and pulled them open here anew. As the world thus filled and emptied its lungs, the same breath ended a few seconds away and then, a little further off, took up again the theme of a fugue that stone and air were playing on a world-scale. Each time, the theme was repeated in a slightly lower key. As I followed it into the distance, I became a little calmer. Reaching the end of so stirring a vision, with one final glance I took in the whole range of hills breathing in unison as they slipped away, as if in some song of the entire earth.

Millions of eyes, I knew, had gazed at this landscape, and for me it was like the first smile of the sky. It took me out of myself in the deepest sense of the word. It assured me that but for my love and the wondrous cry of these stones, there was no meaning in anything. The world is beautiful, and outside it there is no salvation. The great truth that it patiently taught me is that the mind is nothing, nor even the heart. And that the stone warmed by the sun or the cypress tree shooting up against the suddenly clear sky mark the limits of the only universe in which "being right" is meaningful: nature without men. And this world annihilates me. It carries me to the end. It denies me without anger. As that evening fell over Florence, I was moving toward a wisdom where everything had already been overcome, except that tears came into my eyes and a great sob of poetry welling up within me made me forget the world's truth.

It is on this moment of balance I must end: the strange moment when spirituality rejects ethics, when happiness springs from the absence of hope, when the mind finds its justification in the body. If it is true that every truth carries its bitterness within, it is also true that every denial contains a flourish of affirmations. And this song of hopeless love born in contemplation may also seem the most effective guide for action. As he emerges from the tomb, the risen Christ of Piero della Francesca has no human expression on his face—only a fierce and soulless grandeur that I cannot help taking for a resolve to live. For the wise man, like the idiot, expresses little. The reversion delights me.

But do I owe this lesson to Italy, or have I drawn it from my own heart? It was surely in Italy that I became aware of it. But this is because Italy, like other privileged places, offers me the spectacle of a beauty in which, nonetheless, men die. Here again truth must decay, and what is more exalting? Even if I long for it, what have I in common with a truth that is not destined to decay? It is not on my scale. And to love it would be pretense. People rarely understand that it is never through despair that a man gives up what constituted his life. Impulses and moments of despair lead toward other lives and merely indicate a quivering attachment to the lessons of the earth. But it can happen that when he reaches a certain degree of lucidity a man feels his heart is closed, and without protest or rebellion turns his back on what up to then he had taken for his life, that is to say, his restlessness. If Rimbaud dies in Abyssinia without having written a single line, it is not because he prefers adventure or has renounced literature. It is because "that's how things are," and because when we reach a certain stage of awareness we finally acknowledge something which each of us, according to our particular vocation, seeks not to understand. This clearly involves undertaking the survey of a certain desert. But this strange desert is accessible only to those who can live there in the full anguish of their thirst.

Then, and only then, is it peopled with the living waters of happiness.

Within reach of my hand, in the Boboli gardens, hung enormous golden Chinese persimmons whose bursting skin oozed a thick syrup. Between this light hill and these juicy fruits, between the secret brotherhood linking me to the world and the hunger urging me to seize the orange-colored flesh above my hand, I could feel the tension that leads certain men from asceticism to sensual delights and from self-denial to the fullness of desire. I used to wonder, I still wonder at this bond that unites man with the world, this double image in which my heart can intervene and dictate its happiness up to the precise limit where the world can either fulfill or destroy it. Florence! One of the few places in Europe where I have understood that at the heart of my revolt consent is dormant. In its sky mingled with tears and sunlight, I learned to consent to the earth and be consumed in the dark flame of its celebrations. I felt . . . but what word can I use? What excess? How can one consecrate the harmony of love and revolt? The earth! In this great temple deserted by the gods, all my idols have feet of clay.

III

Summer

1954

(*L'Eté*)

But you, you were born for a limpid day.
                                            —Hölderlin

The Minotaur,
or Stopping in Oran

to Pierre Galindo

This essay dates from 1939—something the reader should hear in mind in judging what Oran might be like today. Violent protests emanating from this beautiful town have in fact assured me that all the imperfections have been (or will be) remedied. The beauties celebrated in this essay, have, on the other hand, been jealously protected. Oran, a happy and realistic city, no longer needs writers. It is waiting for tourists.

(1953)

There are no more deserts. There are no more islands. Yet one still feels the need of them. To understand this world, one must sometimes turn away from it; to serve men better, one must briefly hold them at a distance. But where can the necessary solitude be found, the long breathing space in which the mind gathers its strength and takes stock of its courage? There are still the great cities. But they must meet certain conditions.

The cities Europe offers are too full of murmurs from the past. A practiced ear can still detect the rustling of wings, the quivering of souls. We feel the dizziness of the centuries, of glory and revolutions. We are reminded of the clamor in which Europe was forged. There is not enough silence.

Paris is often a desert for the heart, but sometimes, from the height of Père-Lachaise, a wind of revolution suddenly fills this desert with flags and vanquished grandeurs. The same is true of certain Spanish towns, of Florence or Prague. Salzburg would be peaceful without Mozart. But now and then the great cry of Don Juan plunging into hell runs across the Salzach. Vienna seems more silent, a maiden among cities. Its stones are no more than three centuries old, and their youth has known no sadness. But Vienna stands at a crossroads of history. The clash of empires echoes around her. On certain evenings when the sky clothes itself in blood, the stone horses on the monuments of the Ring seem about to take flight. In this fleeting instant, when everything speaks of power and history, you can distinctly hear the Ottoman empire crashing under the charge of the Polish cavalry. Here, too, there is not enough silence.

It is certainly this well-populated solitude that men look for in the cities of Europe. At least, men who know what they want. Here, they can choose their company, take it and leave it. How many minds have been tempered in the walk between a hotel room and the old stones of the Île Saint-Louis! It is true that others died of loneliness. But it was here, in any case, that those who survived found reasons to grow and for self-affirmation. They were alone and yet not alone. Centuries of history and beauty, the burning evidence of a thousand past lives, accompanied them along the Seine and spoke to them both of traditions and of conquests. But their youth urged them to call forth this company. There comes a time, there come times in history, when such company is a nuisance. "It's between the two of us now," cries Rastignac as he confronts the vast mustiness of Paris. Yes, but two can also be too many!

Deserts themselves have taken on a meaning; poetry has handicapped them. They have become the sacred places for all the world's suffering. What the heart requires at certain moments is just the opposite, a place without poetry. Descartes, for his meditations, chose as his desert the busiest commercial city of his time. There he found his solitude, and the chance to write what is perhaps the greatest of our virile poems: "The first (precept) was never to accept anything as true unless I knew without the slightest doubt that it was so." One can have less ambition and yet the same longing. But for the last three centuries Amsterdam has been covered with museums. To escape from poetry and rediscover the peacefulness of stones we need other deserts, and other places without soul or resources. Oran is one of these.

The Street

I have often heard people from Oran complain about their town: "There are no interesting people here." But you wouldn't want them if there were! A number of high-minded people have tried to acclimate this desert to the customs of another world, faithful to the principle that no one can genuinely serve art or ideas without cooperation from others.* The result is that the only edifying circles are those of poker players, boxing and bowling fans, and local clubs. At least their atmosphere is natural. After all, there is a kind of greatness that doesn't lend itself to elevation. It is sterile by nature. And anyone who wants to find it leaves the clubs behind to descend into the street.

The streets of Oran are reserved for dust, pebbles, and heat. If it rains there is a flood and a sea of mud. But rain or shine, the shops have the same absurd, extravagant look. All the bad taste of Europe and the Orient meets in Oran. There, pell-mell, are marble greyhounds, Swan Lake ballet dancers, Diana the Huntress in green galalith, discus throwers and harvesters, everything that serves as wedding or birthday presents, the whole depressing crew that some joker of a businessman endlessly conjures up to fill our mantelpieces. But the relentless bad taste reaches a point of baroque extravagance where all can be forgiven. Behold, embellished with dust, the contents of one shop window: ghastly plaster-cast models of tortured feet, a batch of

---

*In Oran, you meet Gogol's Klestakoff. He yawns and then says: "I feel we ought to concern ourselves with higher things."

Rembrandt sketches "given away at 150 francs each," a quantity of "practical jokes and tricks," tricolor wallets, an eighteenth-century pastel drawing, a mechanical plush donkey, bottles of *eau de Provence* for preserving green olives, and a wretched wooden Virgin with an indecent smile. (So that no one will be left in ignorance, the management has placed a label at its feet: "Wooden Virgin.")

You can find in Oran:

1. Cafés whose grease-covered countertops are strewn with the feet and wings of flies, where the proprietor never stops smiling although the place is always empty. A "small black coffee" used to cost twelve sous and a "large" eighteen;

2. Photographers' shops where techniques have not progressed since the invention of sensitized paper. They display a singular fauna, never encountered in the street, ranging from a pseudo sailor leaning with one elbow on a console table to a marriageable maiden in a dowdy dress, simpering with dangling arms against a sylvan background. It can be assumed that these are not copies from nature but original creations;

3. An edifying abundance of undertakers. This is not because more people die in Oran than elsewhere,

but simply, I suppose, because they make more fuss about it.

The endearing simplicity of this nation of shopkeepers even extends to their advertising. The program of a local movie theater describes a third-rate coming attraction. I note the adjectives "magnificent," "splendid," "extraordinary," "marvelous," "overwhelming," and "stupendous." In conclusion, the management informs the public of the considerable sacrifices it has had to make in order to be able to present this astonishing production. The price of seats, however, will remain the same.

It would be wrong to assume that this merely shows the taste for exaggeration peculiar to Mediterranean countries. What the authors of this remarkable advertisement are really doing is giving proof of their psychological perspicacity. They need to overcome the indifference and profound apathy people have in this country when faced with a choice between two entertainments, two jobs, and often, even between two women. One decides only when compelled to do so. And the advertisers are perfectly aware of this. They will go to American extremes, since the same exasperating conditions exist in both places.

Finally, the streets of Oran reveal the two main pleasures of the local young people: having their shoes shined, and promenading in these same shoes along the boulevard. To understand fully the first of these two sensual delights, you must entrust your shoes at ten o'clock on a Sunday morning to the shoe shiners on the boulevard Gallieni. There, perched on a high armchair, one can enjoy the peculiar satisfaction that even the layman derives from the spectacle of men as deeply and visibly in love with their work as are the shoe cleaners of Oran. Everything is worked out to the last detail. Several brushes, three kinds of polishing rags, shoe polish mixed with gasoline: one would think the operation concluded as a perfect shine rises beneath the application of the soft brush. But the same eager hand puts a second coat of polish on the gleaming surface, rubs it, dulls it, drives the cream into the very heart of the leather and then creates, with the same brush, a double and truly definitive shine that flashes forth from the depths.

The marvels thus obtained are then exhibited to the connoisseurs. To really appreciate the pleasures offered by the boulevard, you must attend the costume balls organized by the young people of Oran every evening in the town's main thoroughfares. "Fashionable" Oranians between the ages of sixteen and twenty model their elegance on American movie stars, disguising themselves every night before dinner. With curly, brilliantined hair flowing from under a felt hat pulled down over the left ear while its brim obliterates the right eye, the neck encircled in a collar generous enough to receive the continuation of the hair, the microscopic knot of the tie held in place by the strictest of pins, a jacket hanging half way down the thighs and nipped in at the hips, light-colored trousers hanging short, and shoes gleaming above triple soles, these youths click along the sidewalks, sounding their unshakable self-confidence with their steel-tipped shoes. In every detail they attempt to imitate the style, the brashness, the superiority of Mr. Clark Gable. This is why, thanks to their rather careless pronunciation, the town's more critical citizens have nicknamed these young men "The Clarques."

In any case, the main boulevards of Oran are invaded late every afternoon by an army of amiable adolescents who take the greatest pains to look like gangsters. Since the young girls know they have been destined since birth to marry these tender-hearted ruffians, they too flaunt the make-up and elegance of the great American actresses. The same cynics consequently christen them "Marlenes." Thus, when on the evening boulevards the chirping of birds rises from the palm trees to the sky, scores of Clarques and Marlenes meet, and size each other up appreciatively, happy to be alive and to make believe, indulging for an hour in the bliss of perfect existences. What we are witnessing here, to quote the envious, are meetings of the American delegation. The words reveal the bitterness of those over thirty who have no part in such games. They fail to see these daily congresses of youth and romantic love for what they are— the parliaments of birds one finds in Hindu literature. But no one, on the boulevards of Oran, discusses the problem of Being, or worries about the way to perfection. There is only the fluttering of wings, the flaunting of outspread tails, flirtations between victorious graces, all the rapture of a careless song that fades with the coming of night.

Already I hear Klestakoff: "We must concern ourselves with higher things." Alas, he is quite capable of doing so. A little encouragement, and in a few years time he will populate this desert. But, for the time being, a slightly secretive soul can find deliverance in this facile town, with its parade of made-up maidens so incapable of ready-made emotion that the ruse of their borrowed coquetry is immediately uncovered. Concern ourselves with higher things! We would do better to use our eyes: Santa Cruz carved out of the rock, the mountains, the flat sea, the violent wind and the sun, the tall cranes in the docks, the sheds, the quays, and the gigantic flights of stairs that scale the rock on which the town is set, and in the town itself the games and the boredom, the tumult and the solitude. Perhaps none of this is elevated enough. But the great value of such overpopulated islands is that in them the heart can strip itself bare. Silence is possible now only in noisy towns. From Amsterdam, Descartes writes the aging Guez de Balzac, "I go walking every day in the confusion of a great people, with as much freedom and quiet as you must find in your country lanes."

The Desert in Oran

Compelled to live facing a glorious landscape, the people of Oran have overcome this formidable handicap by surrounding themselves with extremely ugly buildings. You expect a town opening on the sea, washed and refreshed by the evening breezes. But except for the Spanish district,* you find a city with its back to the sea, built turning in upon itself, like a snail. Oran is a long circular yellow wall,

---

*And the new boulevard Front-de-Mer.

topped by a hard sky. At first, one wanders around the labyrinth, looking for the sea as for Ariadne's sign. But one turns around and around in the stifling yellow streets. In the end, the Oranians are devoured by the Minotaur of boredom. The Oranians have long since stopped wandering. They have let the monster eat them.

No one can know what stone is all about until he has been to Oran. In this dustiest of cities, the pebble is king. It is so much revered that merchants display it in their windows, either as a paperweight or simply for its appearance. People pile them up along the streets, doubtless for pure visual pleasure, since a year later the pile is still there. Things which elsewhere derive their poetry from being green here take on a face of stone. The hundred or so trees that can be found in the business section of the town have been carefully covered with dust. They are a petrified forest, their branches exuding an acrid, dusty smell. In Algiers, the Arab cemeteries have the gentleness they are known for. In Oran, above the Ras-el-Aïn ravine, facing the sea for once, laid out against the blue sky are fields of chalky, crumbly pebbles set blindingly on fire by the sun. In the midst of these dead bones of the earth, here and there a crimson geranium lends its life and fresh blood to the landscape. The whole town is held fast in a stone vise. Seen from the Planters, the cliffs that hold it in their grip are so thick that the landscape loses its reality in so much mineral. Man is an outlaw. So much heavy beauty seems to come from another world.

If one can define the desert as a place with no soul where

the sky alone is king, then Oran awaits its prophets. All around and above the town Africa's brutal nature is resplendent in its burning glory. It shatters the ill-chosen décor men have laid upon it, thrusting its violent cries between each house and down on all the rooftops. As one climbs one of the roads along the side of Santa Cruz mountain, what appears at first are the scattered, brightly colored cubes of Oran. A bit higher, and already the jagged cliffs surrounding the plateau crouch into the sea like red beasts. A little higher still and great whirlpools of sun and wind blanket the untidy town, blowing and battering through its scattered confusion in all four corners of the rocky landscape. Confronted here are man's magnificent anarchy and the permanence of an unchanging sea. Enough to raise along the mountain road a mounting, overwhelming scent of life.

There is something implacable about deserts. The mineral sky of Oran, its trees and streets coated with dust unite to create this thick, impassive world in which the mind and heart are never diverted from themselves or their single subject, which is man. I am speaking here of difficult retreats. People write books about Florence and Athens. These towns have formed so many European minds that they must have a meaning. They maintain the power to sadden or excite. They calm a certain hunger of the soul whose proper food is memory. But how can one feel tender in a town where nothing appeals to the mind, where even ugliness is anonymous, where the past is reduced to nothing? Emptiness, boredom, an indifferent sky: what enticements do these places offer? Solitude, doubt, and perhaps human beings. For a certain race of men, human beings, wherever they are beautiful, are a bitter homeland. Oran is one of the thousand capitals such men possess.

Sports

The Central Sporting Club, in the rue du Fondouk, in Oran, is presenting an evening of boxing, which it claims will be appreciated by those who really love the sport. What this actually means is that the boxers whose names are on the posters are far from being champions, that some of them will be stepping into the ring for the first time, and that you can therefore count on the courage, if not the skill, of the contestants. Electrified by an Oranian's promise that "blood will flow," I find myself this evening among the real lovers of the sport.

It would appear that the fans never demand comfort. A ring has been erected at the far end of a kind of whitewashed, garishly lit garage, with a corrugated iron roof. Folding chairs have been set up on all four sides of the ropes. These are the "ringside seats." Other seats have been set up the length of the hall, and at the far end there is a wide open space known as the "promenade," so named because not one of the five hundred people standing there can take out his pocket handkerchief without causing a serious accident. A thousand men and two or three women—of the type who, according to my neighbor, "always want to show off"—are breathing in this rectangular box. Everyone is sweating ferociously. While we wait for the young hopefuls to step into the ring, an immense loudspeaker grinds out Tino Rossi. Ballads before butchery.

The true fan has limitless patience. The match scheduled for nine o'clock has not yet started at half past, and yet no one complains. It is a warm spring evening, and the smell of men in shirt sleeves is intoxicating. Vigorous discussions are punctuated with the periodic popping of lemonade corks and the tireless lamentations of the Corsican singer. A few late arrivals squeeze into the audience as a spotlight rains blinding light on the ring. The amateur fights begin.

These "white hopes," or beginners, who fight for pleasure, are always anxious to prove it by massacring each other at the first opportunity, with a fine disregard for technique. None of them has ever lasted more than three rounds. Tonight's hero is a certain "Kid Avion," who ordinarily sells lottery tickets on café terraces. At the beginning of the second round, his opponent took an unfortunate dive out of the ring under the impact of a propellerlike fist.

The crowd has grown a little more excited, though still polite. Gravely, it inhales the sacred scent of liniment. It contemplates this series of slow rites and confused sacrifices, rendered even more authentic by the expiatory patterns thrown against the whiteness of the wall by the struggling shadows. These are the formal prologue of a savage and calculated religion. Only later comes the trance.

And, at this very moment, the loudspeaker introduces Amar, "the hometown tough who has never surrendered," against Pérez, "the Algerian puncher." An outsider might well misinterpret the howls that greet the presentation of the boxers in the ring. He would imagine this was some sensational fight in which the two rivals were going to settle a personal quarrel well known to the public. It is, indeed, a quarrel that they are going to settle, but one that, for the last hundred years, has mortally divided Algiers and Oran. A few hundred years ago, these two North African towns would already have bled each other white, as Florence and Pisa did in happier times. Their rivalry is all the stronger for being based on absolutely nothing. Having every reason to love each other, they hate all the more intensely. The Oranians accuse the Algerians of being "stuck-up." The Algerians insinuate that Oranians have no manners. Such insults are more scathing than one might think, since they are metaphysical. And, because they cannot besiege each other, Oran and Algiers meet, struggle, and exchange insults in the field of sport and in competition over statistics and public works.

A page of history is therefore unfolding in the ring. And the hometown tough guy, supported by a thousand howling voices, is defending a way of life and the pride of a province against Pérez. Truth compels me to say that Amar is making his points badly. His arguments are out of order: he lacks reach. The Algerian puncher, on the other hand, is long enough in the arm and makes his points persuasively against his opponent's eyebrow. The Oranian flaunts his colors triumphantly, amid the howls of the frenzied spectators. In spite of repeated encouragement from the gallery and from my neighbor, in spite of the fearless "Slug him," "Give him hell," the insidious cries of "foul," "Oh, the referee didn't see it," the optimistic "He's pooped," "He's had it," the Algerian is declared winner on points to the accompaniment of interminable booing. My neighbor, who likes to talk about the sporting spirit, applauds ostentatiously, whispering to me in a voice hoarse from shouting: "They won't be able to say *there* that Oranians are rude."

But in the hall itself a number of unscheduled fights have already broken out. Chairs are brandished in the air, the police force their way through, the excitement is at its height. To calm these good people and contribute to the restoration of silence, the "management" instantly entrusts the loudspeaker with the thunderous march *Sambre-et-Meuse*. For a few moments the hall takes on a wondrous aspect. Confused bunches of fighters and benevolent referees wave to and fro beneath the policemen's grasp, the gallery is delighted and urges them to further efforts with wild cries, cock-a-doodle-doos, or ironic catcalls soon drowned in the irresistible flood of military music.

But the announcement that the main fight is about to start is enough to restore calm. This happens quickly, with no flourishes, the way actors leave the stage as soon as the play is over. In the most natural way in the world, hats are dusted, chairs put back in their place, and every face immediately assumes the benign expression of the respectable spectator who has paid for his seat at a family concert.

In the last fight of the evening a French naval champion confronts an Oranian boxer. This time it is the latter who has the advantage of reach. But in the first few rounds his superiority does not appeal much to the crowd, which is sleeping off its excitement, convalescing. Everyone is still out of breath. The applause seems unfelt; the whistling half-hearted. The spectators split into two camps, as they must do if order is to prevail. But each man's choice yields to the indifference of great weariness. If the Frenchman holds in the clinches, if the Oranian forgets that one does not punch with the head, the boxer is bowled over, by a broadside of hisses but immediately put back on his feet with a salvo of applause. It is not until the seventh round that Sport reappears as the fans begin to rouse from their fatigue. The Frenchman has actually hit the canvas and anxious to regain points has charged at his opponent. "Here we go," says my neighbor. "Now comes the bull-fight." And that is just what it is. Bathed in sweat under the implacable lights, the two boxers open their guard, close their eyes, and swing. They push with their knees and shoulders, exchange blood, and snort with fury. At the same moment, the spectators rise and punctuate each hero's effort. They take the blows, return them, echoing them in a thousand harsh and panting voices. Those who arbitrarily picked their favorite stick stubbornly to their choices, and get passionate about it. Every ten seconds my right ear is pierced by my neighbor's shouting: "Come on, blue-jacket! Get him, sailor," while a spectator in front of us shouts "*Anda, hombre!*" to the Oranian. The hombre and the blue-jacket go to it, egged on in this whitewashed temple of cement and corrugated tin by a crowd completely given over to these low-brow gods. Every dull thud on the gleaming chests echoes in enormous vibrations through the very body of the crowd, who, along with the boxers themselves, give the fight their all.

In this atmosphere, the announcement of a draw is

badly received. It runs contrary to what, in the crowd, is an utterly Manichaean vision: there is good and evil, the winner and the loser. One must be right if one isn't wrong. The result of this impeccable logic is immediately expressed by two thousand energetic lungs accusing the judges of being either bought or sold. But the blue-jacket has embraced his opponent in the ring and drinks in his fraternal sweat. This is enough to make the crowd effect an immediate about-face and burst into applause. My neighbor is right: they are not uncivilized.

The crowd spilling out now into a night filled with silence and stars has just fought the most exhausting land of battle. The people say nothing, they slip furtively away, too exhausted for post-mortems. There is good and evil; this religion is merciless. The cohort of the faithful is now nothing more than a bunch of black and white shadows disappearing into the night. Strength and violence are lonely gods; they do not serve memory. They simply scatter their miraculous fistfuls in the present. They correspond to these people without a past who celebrate their communions around the boxing ring. Their rites are a bit trying, but they simplify everything. Good and evil, the winner and the loser: At Corinth, two temples stood side by side—the Temple of Violence, the Temple of Necessity.

Monuments

For many reasons that have as much to do with economy as with metaphysics, one can say that Oranian style, if such a thing exists, finds clear and forceful expression in that singular edifice known as the *Maison du Colon*. Oran is scarcely lacking in monuments. The city has its quota of Imperial Marshals, ministers, and local benefactors. You come across them in little, dusty squares, as resigned to rain as to sun, converted like everything else to stone and boredom. Yet they represent something imported. In this happy barbarity they are unfortunate traces of civilization.

On the other hand, Oran has raised altars and rostrums in its own honor. Needing a building to house the innumerable agricultural organizations that provide the country a livelihood, they decided to erect it in the most solid materials, placing it at the center of the business district, a convincing representation of their virtues: *La Maison du Colon*. Judging from this building, these virtues are three in number: boldness of taste, love of violence, and a sense of historical synthesis. Egypt, Babylon, and Munich have collaborated in this delicate construction—a large cake resembling an immense inverted cup. Multicolored stones are set along each side of the roof, to the most startling effect. The brightness of the mosaic is so persuasive that all one can discern at first is a shapeless dazzle. But closer inspection reveals a meaning to the fully alerted attention: a gracious settler, in bow tie and sun helmet, is receiving the homage of a procession of slaves clad as nature intended.* Finally, the edifice with all these illuminations has been erected at the center of an intersection, amid the bustle of

---

*As one can see, another quality of the Algerian race is candor.

the tiny gondola-shaped tramways whose squalor is one of the town's charms.

Oran is, moreover, very attached to the two lions that stand in its main square. Since 1888 they have sat majestically on either side of the staircase leading up to the town hall. Their creator was named Caïn. They look imperious and are short in the body. It's said that at night they descend one after the other from their pedestals and pad silently around the darkened square, occasionally stopping to urinate thoughtfully beneath the tall, dusty fig trees. These are rumors, of course, to which Oranians lend an indulgent ear. But the whole thing's unlikely.

Despite some research, I have not been able to develop any great enthusiasm for Caïn. All I have discovered is that he enjoyed a reputation as a skillful depicter of animals. Nonetheless, I often think of him—a tendency the mind acquires in Oran. An artist whose name has a certain echo, who gave this town a work of no importance. Several hundred thousand men have grown familiar with the jovial beasts he placed in front of a pretentious town hall. This is one kind of artistic success. These two lions doubtless bear witness, like thousands of works on the same order, to something quite different from talent. Other men were able to create "The Night Watch," "Saint Francis Receiving the Stigmata," "David," or "The Exaltation of the Flower." Caïn stuck two grinning cats in the town square of a trading province overseas. But David one day will crumble along with Florence, while these lions perhaps will be saved from disaster. Once again, they hint at something further.

Can I clarify this idea? These statues are both insignificant and solid. The mind has made no contribution to them, matter a very large one. Mediocrity seeks to endure by any means, including bronze. We refuse its claims to eternity, but it makes them every day. Isn't mediocrity itself eternity? In any case, there is something touching about this perseverance; it has its lesson, the lesson offered by all Oran's monuments and by the city itself. For an hour a day, once in a while, you are compelled to take an interest in something that is not important. The mind can profit from such moments of calm. This is how it takes the cure, and because these moments of humility are absolutely necessary to the mind, it seems to me this opportunity for mental relaxation is better than many others. Everything perishable seeks to endure. Let's admit that everything wishes to endure. Man's works have no other meaning, and in this respect Caïn's lions have the same chance of success as the ruins at Angkor. This inclines us to be modest.

There are other monuments in Oran, or, at least, that is what we must call them since they too are representative of their town, in perhaps a more significant way. They are the excavations now being made along the coast line for a distance of ten kilometers. The ostensible reason is to transform the brightest of bays into an enormous port. Actually, it is still another opportunity for man to pit himself against stone.

In the canvases of certain Flemish masters, you see the insistent recurrence of an admirably spacious theme: building the Tower of Babel. There are immense landscapes, rocks reaching up into the sky, escarpments teeming with workmen, animals, ladders, strange machines, ropes, and beams. Man is in the picture only to bring out the inhuman vastness of the construction. This is what comes to mind along the coast west of Oran.

Clinging to immense slopes are rails, pick-up trucks, cranes, and miniature railways ... Through whistles, dust, and smoke, toylike locomotives twist around vast blocks of stone under a devouring sun. Night and day a nation of ants swarms over the smoking carcass of the mountain. Scores of men, hanging from the same rope against the cliff face, their bellies pressed to the handles of pneumatic drills, quiver day after day in mid-air, unloosing whole patches of stone that crash down in a roar of dust. Further along, trucks dump their loads from the top of the slopes, and the rocks, suddenly launched toward the sea, roll and dive into the water, each heavy block followed by a shower of lighter stones. At regular intervals, in the dead of night or in the middle of the day, explosions shake the whole mountain and raise the very sea itself.

What man is doing with these excavations is launching a head-on attack against stone. And if we could for a moment forget the harsh slavery that makes this work possible, we would be filled with admiration. These stones, wrenched from the mountain, help man in his designs. They pile up beneath the first waves, gradually emerge, and finally take shape as a jetty that will soon be covered with men and machines daily moving further out to sea. Vast steel jaws gnaw unceasingly at the cliff's belly, swivel round, and disgorge their excess rubble into the sea. As the face of the cliff sinks lower, the whole coast pushes the sea relentlessly backward.

Stone, of course, cannot be destroyed. All one can do is move it around. In any case, it will always outlast the men who use it. For the moment, it supports their determination to act. Even that determination is doubtless quite gratuitous. But to move things around is man's work: he must choose between doing that or doing nothing at all.* Clearly, the Oranians have chosen. For years to come they will keep piling rocks along the coast and into its indifferent bay. In a hundred years, that is to say, tomorrow, they will have to start again. But today these heaps of rock express the men who move in and out among them, their faces masked in dust and sweat. The true monuments of Oran are still its stones.

Ariadne's Stone

The people of Oran, it would seem, are like that friend of Flaubert's who, from his deathbed, cast a last look on this irreplaceable earth and cried out: "Close the window, it's too beautiful." They have closed the window, they have walled themselves in, they have exorcised the landscape. But Le Poittevin died, and the days continued to follow one another just the same. Just as the sea and land beyond the yellow walls of Oran continue their indifferent dialogue. This permanence in the world has always had a charm for man. It excites him and drives him to despair. The world never has more than one thing to say; it is interesting, then

*This essay deals with one particular temptation. One must have known it. Then one can act or not act, but knowing what the terms are.

boring. But, in the long run, it triumphs through obstinacy. It is always right.

At the very gates of Oran, nature speaks more insistently. Immense stretches of wasteland, covered with fragrant brush, lie in the direction of Canastel. There, the wind and sun speak only of solitude. Rising over Oran is Santa Cruz Mountain, with its plateau and the thousand ravines leading to it. Roads once traveled by coaches cling against the hillsides overlooking the sea. In January, some are covered with flowers. Buttercups and daisies transform them into sumptuous paths, embroidered in white and yellow. Enough has been said about Santa Cruz. But if I had to describe it, I would forget the sacred processions climbing its harsh slopes on great feast days to evoke other pilgrims who find their way in solitude through the red stones, mounting above the motionless bay, to consecrate one perfect, luminous hour to its bareness.

Oran also has deserts of sand: its beaches. The ones near the city gates are empty only in winter and in spring. They are plateaus then, covered with asphodels, and dotted with small, bare villas among the flowers. Below them growls the sea. Yet the sun, the slight wind, the whiteness of the asphodels, the harsh blue of the sky already foreshadow the summer and the golden youth swarming over the beach, long hours on the sand, and the sudden gentleness of evening. Each year there is a new harvest of flower maidens on these shores. Apparently, they only last the season. The next year other warm blossoms, still little girls with bodies hard as buds the summer before, take their place. Descending from the plateau at eleven in the morning, all this young flesh, scarcely covered by its motley garments, flows across the sand like a multicolored wave.

One must go farther (yet strangely near the place where two hundred thousand men turn in circles) to find a landscape still virgin: long, empty dunes on which the passage of men has left no other trace than a worm-eaten hut. From time to time, an Arab shepherd leads the black and beige spots of his herd of goats across the top of the dunes. On these beaches in the province of Oran each summer morning feels like the world's first. Each dusk feels like the last, a solemn death proclaimed at sunset by a final light that darkens every shade. The sea is aquamarine, the road the color of dried blood, the beach yellow. Everything vanishes with the green sun; an hour later, the dunes are streaming with moonlight. These are boundless nights beneath a shower of stars. Storms occasionally drift across them, and flashes of lightning shoot along the dunes, turn the sky pale, casting an orange-glow upon the sand or in our eyes.

But this cannot be shared in words. It must be lived. So much solitude and grandeur make these places unforgettable. In the mild early dawn, beyond the small, still black and bitter waves, a new being cleaves the scarcely endurable waters of the night. The memory of these joys holds no regret, and that is how I know that they were good. After so many years, they are still there, somewhere in this heart that finds fidelity so difficult. And I know that today, if I want to go back, the same sky will still pour its cargo of stars and breezes upon the deserted dunes. These are the lands of innocence.

But innocence needs sand and stone. And man has forgotten how to live with them. At least, this appears to be the case, since he has enclosed himself in this strange town where boredom slumbers. Yet it is this confrontation which gives Oran its value. The capital of boredom, besieged by innocence and beauty, is hemmed in by an army of as many soldiers as stones. At certain times, though, how tempted one feels in this town to defect to the enemy! How tempting to merge oneself with these stones, to mingle with this burning, impassive universe that challenges history and its agitations! A vain temptation, no doubt. But every man has a deep instinct that is neither for destruction nor creation. Simply the longing to resemble nothing. In the shade of the warm buildings of Oran, on its dusty asphalt, one sometimes hears this invitation. For a while, it seems, minds which yield to it are never disappointed. They have the shades of Eurydice and the sleep of Isis. These are the deserts where thought recovers its strength, the cool hand of evening on a troubled heart. No vigil can be kept upon this Mount of Olives; the mind joins and sanctions the sleeping Apostles. Were they really wrong? They did have their revelation after all.

Think of Sakiamouni in the desert. He spent long years there, crouching motionless and looking up to heaven. The gods themselves envied his wisdom and his fate of stone. Swallows had nested in his stiff and outstretched hands. But, one day, off they flew, following the call of distant lands. And the man who had killed in himself desire and will, glory and sadness, began to weep. And so it is that flowers spring from rock. Yes, let us consent to stone when we must. It too can give us the secret and the rapture that we seek in faces. Of course, it cannot last. But what is there that can? Faces lose their secrets and there we are, reduced once more to the bondage of desire. And if stone can do no more for us than can the human heart, it can at least do just as much.

"To be nothing!" For thousands of years this cry has inspired millions of men to revolt against desire and suffering. Its echoes have traveled over centuries and oceans, coming to rest on the oldest sea in the world. They still reverberate softly against the solid cliffs of Oran. Without knowing it, everyone in this country follows this precept. Of course, it's almost in vain. Nothingness lies within our grasp no more than does the absolute. But since we welcome as evidence of grace the eternal signs revealed in roses or in the suffering of men, let us not reject the rare invitations to sleep the earth offers. These have as much truth as the others.

Here, perhaps, is the Ariadne's thread of this frenzied and somnambulistic city. We acquire the virtues, the wholly provisional virtues, of a certain boredom. To be spared, we must say "yes" to the Minotaur. It is an ancient, fertile wisdom. Above the sea, lying silent at the foot of the red cliffs, we need only to balance ourselves precisely between the two massive headlands, to the right and to the left, that are washed in the clear water. In the chugging of a coast-guard vessel crawling out to sea bathed in radiant light, you can distinctly hear the muffled call of glittering, inhuman forces: the Minotaur's farewell.

It is noon, the day itself stands at a point of balance. His rite accomplished, the traveler receives the price of his deliverance: the little stone, dry and soft as an asphodel, that he picks up on the cliff. For the initiate, the world is no heavier to carry than that stone. The burden of Atlas is easy; all one need do is choose his moment. One realizes then that for an hour, a month, a year, these shores can lend themselves to freedom. They offer the same uncritical welcome to the monk, the civil servant, or the conqueror. There were days when I expected to run into Descartes or Cesare Borgia in the streets of Oran. It didn't happen. But perhaps someone else will be more fortunate than I. A great action, a great undertaking, virile meditation used to call for the solitude of a desert or a convent. It was there that men kept vigil over the weapons of their minds. What better place to keep these vigils now than in the emptiness of a large town built to last a long time in the midst of mindless beauty?

Here is the small stone, soft as an asphodel. It lies at the beginning of everything. Flowers, tears (if you insist), departures and struggles are for tomorrow. In the middle of the journey, when the heavens open their fountains of light into vast, resounding space, the headlands all along the coast look like a fleet of ships impatient to weigh anchor. These heavy galleons of rock and light tremble on their keels as if in preparation for a voyage to the island of the sun. Oh, the mornings in Oran! From high on the plateaus, the swallows swoop down into the immense cauldrons of simmering air. The whole coast is ready for departure, a thrill of adventure runs along it. Tomorrow, perhaps, we shall set sail together.

1939

The Almond Trees

"Do you know," Napoleon once said to Fontanes, "what astounds me most about the world? The impotence of force to establish anything. There are only two powers in the world: the sword and the mind. In the end, the sword is always conquered by the mind."

Conquerors, you see, are sometimes melancholy. They have to pay some price for so much vainglory. But what a hundred years ago was true of the sword is no longer true today of the tank. Conquerors have made progress, and the dismal silence of places without intelligence has been established for years at a time in a lacerated Europe. At the time of the hideous wars of Flanders, Dutch painters could still perhaps paint the cockerels in their farmyards.

The Hundred Years War has likewise been forgotten, and yet the prayers of Silesian mystics still linger in some hearts. But today, things have changed; the painter and the monk have been drafted—we are one with the world. The mind has lost that regal certainty which a conqueror could acknowledge; it exhausts itself now in cursing force, for want of knowing how to master it.

Some noble souls keep on deploring this, saying it is evil. We do not know if it is evil, but we know it is a fact. The conclusion is that we must come to terms with it. All we need know, then, is what we want. And what we want precisely is never again to bow beneath the sword, never again to count force as being in the right unless it is serving the mind.

The task is endless, it's true. But we are here to pursue it. I do not have enough faith in reason to subscribe to a belief in progress or to any philosophy of history. I do believe at least that man's awareness of his destiny has never ceased to advance. We have not overcome our condition, and yet we know it better. We know that we live in contradiction, but we also know that we must refuse this contradiction and do what is needed to reduce it. Our task as men is to find the few principles that will calm the infinite anguish of free souls. We must mend what has been torn apart, make justice imaginable again in a world so obviously unjust, give happiness a meaning once more to peoples poisoned by the misery of the century. Naturally, it is a superhuman task. But superhuman is the term for tasks men take a long time to accomplish, that's all.

Let us know our aims then, holding fast to the mind,

even if force puts on a thoughtful or a comfortable face in order to seduce us. The first thing is not to despair. Let us not listen too much to those who proclaim that the world is at an end. Civilizations do not die so easily, and even if our world were to collapse, it would not have been the first. It is indeed true that we live in tragic times. But too many people confuse tragedy with despair. "Tragedy," Lawrence said, "ought to be a great kick at misery." This is a healthy and immediately applicable thought. There are many things today deserving such a kick.

When I lived in Algiers, I would wait patiently all winter because I knew that in the course of one night, one cold, pure February night, the almond trees of the Vallée des Consuls would be covered with white flowers. I would marvel then at the sight of this fragile snow resisting the rains and the wind from the sea. Yet every year it lasted just long enough to prepare the fruit.

There is no symbol here. We will not win our happiness with symbols. We'll need something more solid. I mean only that sometimes, when life weighs too heavily today in a Europe still full of misery, I turn toward those shining lands where so much strength is still intact. I know them too well not to realize that they are the chosen land where courage and contemplation can live in harmony. Thinking of them teaches me that if we are to save the mind we must ignore its gloomy virtues and celebrate its strength and wonder. Our world is poisoned by its misery, and seems to wallow in it. It has utterly surrendered to that evil which Nietzsche called the spirit of heaviness. Let us not add to this. It is futile to weep over the mind, it is enough to labor for it.

But where are the conquering virtues of the mind? The same Nietzsche listed them as mortal enemies to heaviness of the spirit. For him, they are strength of character, taste, the "world," classical happiness, severe pride, the cold frugality of the wise. More than ever, these virtues are necessary today, and each of us can choose the one that suits him best. Before the vastness of the undertaking, let no one forget strength of character. I don't mean the theatrical kind on political platforms, complete with frowns and threatening gestures. But the kind that through the virtue of its purity and its sap, stands up to all the winds that blow in from the sea. Such is the strength of character that in the winter of the world will prepare the fruit.

1940

Prometheus in the Underworld*

I felt the Gods were lacking as long as there was nothing to oppose them.

—Lucian, *Prometheus in the Caucasus*

What does Prometheus mean to man today? One could doubtless claim this God-defying rebel as the model of contemporary man and his protest thousands of years ago in the deserts of Scythia as culminating in the unparalleled historical convulsion of our day. But, at the same time, something suggests that this victim of persecution is still among us and that we are still deaf to the great cry of human revolt of which he gives the solitary signal.

Modern man indeed endures a multitude of suffering on the narrow surface of this earth; for the man deprived of food and warmth, liberty is merely a luxury that can wait; all he can do is suffer a little more, as if it were only a question of letting liberty and its last witnesses vanish a

*This essay was first published in 1947 by Palimugre, in Paris.

bit more. Prometheus was the hero who loved men enough to give them fire and liberty, technology and art. Today, mankind needs and cares only for technology. We rebel through our machines, holding art and what art implies as an obstacle and a symbol of slavery. But what characterizes Prometheus is that he cannot separate machines from art. He believes that both souls and bodies can be freed at the same time. Man today believes that we must first of all free the body, even if the mind must suffer temporary death. But can the mind die temporarily? Indeed, if Prometheus were to reappear, modern man would treat him as the gods did long ago: they would nail him to a rock, in the name of the very humanism he was the first to symbolize. The hostile voices to insult the defeated victim would be the very ones that echo on the threshold of Aeschylean tragedy: those of Force and Violence.

Am I yielding to the meanness of our times, to naked trees and the winter of the world? But this very nostalgia for light is my justification: it speaks to me of another world, of my true homeland. Does this nostalgia still mean something to some men? The year the war began, I was to board a ship and follow the voyage of Ulysses. At that time, even a young man without money could entertain the extravagant notion of crossing the sea in quest of sunlight. But I did what everyone else did at the time. I did not get on that ship. I took my place in the queue shuffling toward the open mouth of hell. Little by little, we entered. At the first cry of murdered innocence, the door slammed shut behind us. We were in hell, and we have not left it since. For six long years we have been trying to come to terms with it. Now we glimpse the warm ghosts of fortunate islands only at the end of long, cold, sunless years that lie ahead.

How then, in this damp, dark Europe, can we avoid hearing with a quiver of regret and difficult complicity the cry the aged Chateaubriand uttered to Ampère departing for Greece: "You won't find a leaf from the olive trees or a single grape left of the ones I saw in Attica. I even miss the grass that grew there in my day. I haven't had the strength to make a patch of heather grow." And we too, for all our youthful blood, sunk as we are in the terrible old age of this last century, sometimes miss the grass that has always grown, the olive leaf that we'll no longer go to look at just to see it, and the grapes of liberty. Man is everywhere, and everywhere we find his cries, his suffering, and his threats. With so many men gathered together, there is no room for grasshoppers. History is a sterile earth where heather does not grow. Yet men today have chosen history, and they neither could nor should turn away from it. But instead of mastering it, they agree a little more each day to be its slave. Thus they betray Prometheus, this son "both bold in thought and light of heart." This is how they revert to the wretchedness of the men Prometheus tried to save. "They saw without seeing, heard without listening, like figures in a dream."

Yes, one evening in Provence, one perfect hill, one whiff of salt are enough to show us that everything still lies before us. We need to invent fire once more, to settle down once again to the job of appeasing the body's hunger. Attica, liberty, and its grape-gathering, the bread of the soul, must come later. What can we do about this but cry to ourselves: "They will never exist any more, or they will exist for others," and do what must be done so that others at least do not go begging? We who feel this so painfully, and yet who try to accept it without bitterness, are we lagging behind, or are we forging ahead, and will we have the strength to make the heather grow again?

We can imagine how Prometheus would have replied to this question that rises from our century. Indeed, he has already given his answer: "I promise you, O mortals, both improvement and repair, if you are skillful, virtuous and strong enough to achieve them with your own hands." If, then, it is true that salvation lies in our own hands, I will answer Yes to the question of the century, because of the thoughtful strength and the intelligent courage I still feel in some of the people I know. "O Justice, O my mother," cries Prometheus, "you see what I am made to suffer." And Hermes mocks the hero: "I am amazed that, being a God, you did not foresee the torment you are suffering." "I did see it," replies the rebel. The men I've mentioned are also the sons of justice. They, too, suffer from the misery of all men, knowing what they do. They know all too well that blind justice does not exist, that history has no eyes, and that we must therefore reject its justice in order to replace it as much as possible with the justice conceived by the mind. This is how Prometheus returns in our century.

Myths have no life of their own. They wait for us to give them flesh. If one man in the world answers their call, they give us their strength in all its fullness. We must preserve this myth, and ensure that its slumber is not mortal so that its resurrection is possible. I sometimes doubt whether men can be saved today. But it is still possible to save their children, both body and mind. It is possible to offer them at the same time the chance for happiness and beauty. If we must resign ourselves to living without beauty, and the freedom that is a part of beauty, the myth of Prometheus is one of those that will remind us that any mutilation of man can only be temporary, and that one serves nothing in man if one does not serve the whole man. If he is hungry for bread and heather, and if it is true that bread is the more necessary, let us learn how to keep the memory of heather alive. At the darkest heart of history, Promethean men, without flinching from their difficult calling, will keep watch over the earth and the tireless grass. In the thunder and lightning of the gods, the chained hero keeps his quiet faith in man. This is how he is harder than his rock and more patient than his vulture. His long stubbornness has more meaning for us than his revolt against the gods. Along with his admirable determination to separate and exclude nothing, which always has and always will reconcile humanity's suffering with the springtimes of the world.

1946

A Short Guide to Towns Without a Past

The softness of Algiers is rather Italian. The cruel glare of Oran has something Spanish about it. Constantine, perched high on a rock above the Rummel Gorges, is reminiscent of Toledo. But Spain and Italy overflow with memories, with works of art and exemplary ruins. Toledo has had its El Greco and its Barrès. The cities I speak of, on the other hand, are towns without a past. Thus they are without tenderness or abandon. During the boredom of the siesta hours, their sadness is implacable and has no melancholy. In the morning light, or in the natural luxury of the evenings, their delights are equally ungentle. These towns give nothing to the mind and everything to the passions. They are suited neither to wisdom nor to the delicacies of taste. A Barrès or anyone like him would be completely pulverized.

Travelers with a passion for other people's passions, oversensitive souls, aesthetes, and newlyweds have nothing to gain from going to Algiers. And, unless he had a divine call, a man would be ill-advised to retire and live there forever. Sometimes, in Paris, when people I respect ask me about Algeria, I feel like crying out: "Don't go there." Such joking has some truth in it. For I can see what they are expecting and know they will not find it. And, at the same time, I know the attractions and the subtle power of this country, its insinuating hold on those who linger, how it immobilizes them first by ridding them of questions and finally by lulling them to sleep with its everyday life. At first the revelation of the light, so glaring that everything turns black and white, is almost suffocating. One gives way to it, settles down in it, and then realizes that this protracted splendor gives nothing to the soul and is merely an excessive delight. Then one would like to return to the mind. But the men of this country—and this is their strength—seem to have more heart than mind. They can be your friends (and what friends!), but you can never tell them your secrets. This might be considered dangerous here in Paris, where souls are poured out so extravagantly and where the water of secrets flows softly and endlessly along among the fountains, the statues, and the gardens.

This land most resembles Spain. With no traditions Spain would be merely a beautiful desert. And unless one happens to have been born there, there is only one race of men who can dream of withdrawing forever to the desert. Having been born in this desert, I can hardly think of describing it as a visitor. Can one catalogue the charms of a woman one loves dearly? No, one loves her all of a piece, if I may use the expression, with one or two precise reasons for tenderness, like a favorite pout or a particular way of shaking the head. Such is my long-standing liaison with Algeria, one that will doubtless never end and that keeps me from being completely lucid. All anyone can do in such a case is to persevere and make a kind of abstract list of what he loves in the thing he loves. This is the kind of academic exercise I can attempt here on the subject of Algeria.

First there is the beauty of the young people. The Arabs, of course, and then the others. The French of Algeria are a bastard race, made up of unexpected mixtures. Spaniards and Alsatians, Italians, Maltese, Jews, and Greeks have met here. As in America, such raw intermingling has had happy results. As you walk through Algiers, look at the wrists of the women and the young men, and then think of the ones you see in the Paris *métro*.

The traveler who is still young will also notice that the women are beautiful. The best place in Algiers to appreciate this is the terrace of the Café des Facultés, in the rue Michelet, on a Sunday morning in April. Groups of young women in sandals and light, brightly colored dresses walk up and down the street. You can admire them without inhibitions: that is what they come for. The Cintra bar, on the boulevard Galliéni in Oran, is also a good observatory. In Constantine, you can always stroll around the bandstand. But since the sea is several hundred kilometers away, there is something missing in the people you meet there. In general, and because of this geographical location, Constantine offers fewer attractions, although the quality of its ennui is rather more delicate.

If the traveler arrives in summer, the first thing to do, obviously, is to go down to the beaches surrounding the towns. He will see the same young people, more dazzling because less clothed. The sun gives them the somnolent eyes of great beasts. In this respect, the beaches of Oran are the finest, for both nature and women are wilder there.

As for the picturesque, Algiers offers an Arab town, Oran a Negro village and a Spanish district, and Constantine a Jewish quarter. Algiers has a long necklace of boulevards along the sea; you must walk there at night. Oran has few trees, but the most beautiful stone in the world. Constantine has a suspension bridge where the thing to do is have your photograph taken. On very windy days, the bridge sways to and fro above the deep gorges of the Rummel, and you have the feeling of danger.

I recommend that the sensitive traveler, if he goes to Algiers, drink *anisette* under the archways around the harbor, go to La Pêcherie in the morning and eat freshly caught fish grilled on charcoal stoves; listen to Arab music in a little café on the rue de la Lyre whose name I've forgotten; sit on the ground, at six in the evening, at the foot of the statue of the duc d'Orléans, in Government Square (not for the sake of the duke, but because there are people walking by, and it's pleasant there); have lunch at Padovani's, which is a kind of dance hall on stilts along the seashore, where the life is always easy; visit the Arab cemeteries, first to find calm and beauty there, then to appreciate at their true value the ignoble cities where we stack our dead; go and smoke a cigarette in the Casbah on the rue des Bouchers, in the midst of spleens, livers, lungs, and intestines that drip blood on everything (the cigarette is necessary, these medieval practices have a strong smell).

As to the rest, you must be able to speak ill of Algiers when in Oran (insist on the commercial superiority of Oran's harbor), make fun of Oran when in Algiers (don't hesitate to accept the notion that Oranians "don't know how to live"), and, at every opportunity, humbly acknowledge the surpassing merit of Algiers in comparison to metropolitan France. Once these concessions have been made, you will be able to appreciate the real superiority of the Algerian over the Frenchman—that is to say, his limitless generosity and his natural hospitality.

And now perhaps I can stop being ironic. After all, the best way to speak of what one loves is to speak of it lightly. When Algeria is concerned, I am always afraid to pluck the inner cord it touches in me, whose blind and serious song I know so well. But at least I can say that it is my true country, and that anywhere in the world I recognize its sons and my brothers by the friendly laughter that fills me at the sight of them. Yes, what I love about the cities of Algeria is not separate from their inhabitants. That is why I like it best there in the evening when the shops and offices pour into the still, dim streets a chattering crowd that runs right up to the boulevards facing the sea and starts to grow silent there, as night falls and the lights from the sky, from the lighthouses in the bay, and from the streetlamps merge together little by little into a single flickering glow. A whole people stands meditating on the seashore then, a thousand solitudes springing up from the crowd. Then the vast African nights begin, the royal exile, and the celebration of despair that awaits the solitary traveler.

No, you must certainly not go there if you have a lukewarm heart or if your soul is weak and weary! But for those who know what it is to be torn between yes and no, between noon and midnight, between revolt and love, and for those who love funeral pyres along the shore, a flame lies waiting in Algeria.

1947

Helen's Exile

The Mediterranean has a solar tragedy that has nothing to do with mists. There are evenings, at the foot of mountains by the sea, when night falls on the perfect curve of a little bay and an anguished fullness rises from the silent waters. Such moments make one realize that if the Greeks knew despair, they experienced it always through beauty and its oppressive quality. In this golden sadness, tragedy reaches its highest point. But the despair of our world—quite the opposite—has fed on ugliness and upheavals. That is why Europe would be ignoble if suffering ever could be.

We have exiled beauty; the Greeks took arms for it. A basic difference—but one that goes far back. Greek thought was always based on the idea of limits. Nothing was carried to extremes, neither religion nor reason, because Greek thought denied nothing, neither reason nor religion. It gave everything its share, balancing light with shade. But the Europe we know, eager for the conquest of totality, is the daughter of excess. We deny beauty, as we deny everything that we do not extol. And, even though we do it in diverse ways, we extol one thing and one alone: a future world in which reason will reign supreme. In our madness, we push back the eternal limits, and at once dark Furies swoop down upon us to destroy. Nemesis, goddess of moderation, not of vengeance, is watching. She chastises, ruthlessly, all those who go beyond the limit.

The Greeks, who spent centuries asking themselves what was just, would understand nothing of our idea of justice. Equity, for them, supposed a limit, while our whole continent is convulsed by the quest for a justice we see as absolute. At the dawn of Greek thought Heraclitus already conceived justice as setting limits even upon the physical universe itself: "The sun will not go beyond its bounds, for otherwise the Furies who watch over justice will find it out." We, who have thrown both universe and mind out of orbit, find such threats amusing. In a drunken sky we ignite the suns that suit us. But limits nonetheless exist and we know it. In our wildest madness we dream of an equilibrium we have lost, and which in our simplicity we think we shall discover once again when our errors cease—an infantile presumption, which justifies the fact that childish peoples, inheriting our madness, are managing our history today.

A fragment attributed to the same Heraclitus states simply: "Presumption, regression of progress." And centuries after the Ephesian, Socrates, threatened by the death penalty, granted himself no superiority other than this: he did not presume to know what he did not know. The most exemplary life and thought of these centuries ends with a proud acknowledgment of ignorance. In forgetting this we have forgotten our virility. We have preferred the power that apes greatness—Alexander first of all, and then the Roman conquerors, whom our school history books, in an incomparable vulgarity of soul, teach us to admire. We have conquered in our turn, have set aside the bounds, mastered heaven and earth. Our reason has swept everything away. Alone at last, we build our empire upon a desert. How then could we conceive that higher balance in which nature balanced history, beauty, and goodness, and which brought the music of numbers even into the tragedy of blood? We turn our back on nature, we are ashamed of beauty. Our miserable tragedies have the smell of an office, and their blood is the color of dirty ink.

That is why it is indecent to proclaim today that we are the sons of Greece. Or, if we are, we are sons turned renegade. Putting history on the throne of God, we are marching toward theocracy, like those the Greeks called barbarians, whom they fought to the death in the waters of Salamis. If we really want to grasp the difference, we must look to the one man among our philosophers who is the true rival of Plato. "Only the modern city," Hegel dares to write, "offers the mind the grounds on which it can achieve awareness of itself." We live in the time of great cities. The world has been deliberately cut off from what gives it permanence: nature, the sea, hills, evening meditations. There is no consciousness any more except in the streets because there is history only in the streets, so runs the decree. And, consequently, our most significant works demonstrate the same prejudice. One looks in vain for landscapes in the major European writers since Dostoevski. History explains neither the natural universe which came before it, nor beauty which stands above it. Consequently it has chosen to ignore them. Whereas Plato incorporated everything—nonsense, reason, and myths—our philosophers admit nothing but nonsense or reason, because they have closed their eyes to the rest. The mole is meditating.

It was Christianity that began to replace the contemplation of the world with the tragedy of the soul. But Christianity at least referred to a spiritual nature, and therefore maintained a certain fixity. Now that God is dead, all that remains are history and power. For a long time now, the whole effort of our philosophers has been solely to replace the idea of human nature with the idea of situation and ancient harmony with the disorderly outbursts of chance or the pitiless movement of reason. While the Greeks used reason to restrain the will, we have ended by placing the impulse of the will at the heart of reason, and reason has therefore become murderous. For the Greeks, values existed a priori and marked out the exact limits of every action. Modern philosophy places its values at the completion of action. They are not, but they become, and we shall know them completely only at the end of history. When they disappear, limits vanish as well, and since ideas differ as to what these values will be, since there is no struggle which, unhindered by these same values, does not extend indefinitely, we are now witnessing the Messianic forces confronting one another, their clamors merging in the shock of empires. Excess is a fire, according to Heraclitus. The fire is gaining ground; Nietzsche has been overtaken. It is no longer with hammer blows but with cannon shots that Europe philosophizes.

Nature is still there, nevertheless. Her calm skies and her reason oppose the folly of men. Until the atom too bursts into flame, and history ends in the triumph of reason and the death agony of the species. But the Greeks never said that the limit could not be crossed. They said it existed and that the man who dared ignore it was mercilessly struck down. Nothing in today's history can contradict them.

Both the historical mind and the artist seek to remake the world. But the artist, through an obligation of his very nature, recognizes limits the historical mind ignores. This is why the latter aims at tyranny while the passion of the artist is liberty. All those who struggle today for liberty are in the final analysis fighting for beauty. Of course, no one thinks of defending beauty solely for its own sake. Beauty cannot do without man, and we shall give our time its greatness and serenity only by sharing in its misery. We shall never again stand alone. But it is equally true that man cannot do without beauty, and this is what our time seems to want to forget. We tense ourselves to achieve empires and the absolute, seek to transfigure the world before having exhausted it, to set it to rights before having understood it. Whatever we may say, we are turning our backs on this world. Ulysses, on Calypso's island, is given the choice between immortality and the land of his fathers. He chooses this earth, and death with it. Such simple greatness is foreign to our minds today. Others will say that we lack humility, but the word, all things considered, is ambiguous. Like Dostoevski's buffoons who boast of everything, rise up to the stars and end by flaunting their shame in the first public place, we simply lack the pride of the man who is faithful to his limitations—that is, the clairvoyant love of his human condition.

"I hate my time," wrote Saint-Exupéry before his death, for reasons that are not far removed from those I have mentioned. But, however overwhelming his cry may be, coming from someone who loved men for their admirable qualities, we shall not take it as our own. Yet what a temptation, at certain times, to turn our backs on this gaunt and gloomy world. But this is our time and we cannot live hating ourselves. It has fallen so low as much from the excess of its virtues as from the greatness of its faults. We shall fight for the one among its virtues that has ancient roots. Which virtue? Patroclus's horses weep for their master, dead in battle. All is lost. But Achilles takes up the battle and victory comes at the end because friendship has been murdered: friendship is a virtue.

It is by acknowledging our ignorance, refusing to be fanatics, recognizing the world's limits and man's, through the faces of those we love, in short, by means of beauty—this is how we may rejoin the Greeks. In a way, the meaning of tomorrow's history is not what people think. It is in the struggle between creation and the inquisition. Whatever the price artists will have to pay for their empty hands, we can hope for their victory. Once again, the philosophy of darkness will dissolve above the dazzling sea. Oh, noonday thought, the Trojan war is fought far from the battleground! Once again, the terrible walls of the modern city will fall, to deliver Helen's beauty, "its soul serene as the untroubled waves."

1948

The Enigma

Waves of sunlight, pouring from the topmost sky, bounce fiercely on the countryside around us. Everything grows quiet beneath its force, and Mount Luberon, over there, is merely a vast block of silence that I listen to unceasingly. I listen carefully, someone is running toward me in the distance, invisible friends call to me, my joy grows, just as years ago. Once again, a happy enigma helps me to understand everything.

Where is the absurdity of the world? Is it this resplendent glow or the memory of its absence? With so much sun in my memory, how could I have wagered on nonsense? People around me are amazed; so am I, at times. I could tell them, as I tell myself, that it was in fact the sun that helped me, and that the very thickness of its light coagulates the universe and its forms into a dazzling darkness. But there are other ways of saying this, and I should like, faced with the white and black clarity that, for me, has always been the sign of truth, to explain in simple terms what I feel about this absurdity which I know too well to allow anyone to hold forth on it without making certain nuances. The very fact of talking about it, after all, will lead us back to the sun.

No man can say what he is. But sometimes he can say what he is not. Everyone wants the man who is still search-ing to have already reached his conclusions. A thousand voices are already telling him what he has found, and yet he knows that he hasn't found anything. Should he search on and let them talk? Of course. But, from time to time, one must defend himself. I do not know what I am looking for, cautiously I give it a name, I withdraw what I said, I repeat myself, I go backward and forward. Yet people insist I identify my term or terms, once and for all. Then I object; when things have a label aren't they lost already? Here, at least, is what I can try to say.

If I am to believe one of my friends, a man always has two characters: his own, and the one his wife thinks he has. Substitute society for wife and we shall understand how a particular expression, used by a writer to describe a whole context of emotions, can be isolated by the way people comment on it and laid before its author every time he tries to talk about something else. Words are like actions: "Are you the father of this child?" "Yes." "Then he is your son." "It is not as simple as that, not at all!" Thus Gerard de Nerval, one filthy night, hanged himself twice, once for himself because he was unhappy, and a second time for his legend, which now helps some people to live. No one can write about real unhappiness, or about certain moments of happiness, and I shall not try to do so here. But, as far as legends are concerned, we can describe them, and, for a moment at least, believe that we have dispelled them.

A writer writes to a great extent to be read (let's admire those who say they don't, but not believe them). Yet more and more, in France, he writes in order to obtain that final consecration which consists of not being read. In fact, from the moment he can provide the material for a feature article in the popular press, there is every possibility that he will be known to a fairly large number of people who will never read his works because they will be content to know his name and to read what other people write about him. From that point on he will be known (and forgotten) not for what he is, but according to the image a hurried journalist has given of him. To make a name in literature, therefore, it is no longer indispensable to write books. It is enough to be thought of as having written one which the evening papers will have mentioned and which one can fall back on for the rest of one's life.

There is no doubt that such a reputation, great or small, will be undeserved. But what can be done about it? Let us rather admit that the inconvenience may also be beneficial. Doctors know that certain illnesses are desirable: they compensate, in some way, for a functional disorder which, without them, might express itself in some more serious disturbance. Thus there are fortunate constipations and providential attacks of arthritis. The flood of words and hasty judgments, which nowadays drowns all public activity in an ocean of frivolity, at least endows the French writer with a modesty he constantly needs in a nation that, furthermore, gives a disproportionate importance to his calling. To see one's name in two or three newspapers I could mention is so harsh a trial that it must inevitably involve some spiritual benefit. Praise be, then, to a society that teaches us so cheaply, every day, by its very homage, that the greatness it honors is worthless. The louder its noise, the quicker it dies. It evokes the flaxen fires Alexander VI often had burned before him to remind him that the glory of this world vanishes like smoke.

But let's leave irony aside. It is enough to say that an artist must resign himself good humoredly and allow what he knows is an undeserved image of himself to lie about in dentists' waiting rooms and at the hairdresser's. I know a fashionable writer who, according to such sources, supposedly spent every night presiding over Bacchanalian orgies, where nymphs were clothed in nothing but their hair and fauns had gloomy fingernails. One might have wondered how he found the time to write a series of books that fill several library shelves. Like most of his colleagues, this writer actually spends his nights sleeping in order to spend long hours every day at his desk, and drinks Vichy water so as not to strain his liver. This does not prevent the average Frenchman, whose Saharan sobriety and mania for cleanliness are well known, from growing indignant at the idea of our writers teaching people to drink and not to wash. There is no dearth of examples. I personally can furnish an excellent cheap recipe for securing a reputation for austerity. I actually have so weighty a reputation, a source of great amusement to my friends (as far as I'm concerned, it rather makes me blush, since I know how little I deserve it). It's enough, for instance, to decline the honor of dining with a newspaper editor of whom you do not have a high opinion. Even simple decency cannot be imagined except by reference to some twisted sickness of the soul. No one will ever imagine that if you refuse this editor's dinner, it may be not only because you haven't a very high opinion of him, but also because your greatest fear in the world is being bored—and what is more boring than a typical Parisian dinner?

One must therefore submit. But, from time to time, you can try to readjust the sights, and repeat that you can't always be a painter of the absurd and that no one can believe in a literature of despair. Of course, it is always possible to write, or to have written, an essay on the notion of the absurd. But after all, you can also write about incest without necessarily having hurled yourself on your unfortunate sister, and I have nowhere read that Sophocles ever thought of killing his father and dishonoring his mother. The idea that every writer necessarily writes about himself and depicts himself in his books is one of the puerile notions that we have inherited from Romanticism. It is by no means impossible—quite the opposite—that a writer should be interested first and foremost in other people, or in his time, or in well-known myths. Even if he does happen to put himself on stage, it is only very exceptionally that he talks about what he is really like. A man's works often retrace the story of his nostalgias or his temptations, practically never his own history especially when they claim to be autobiographical. No man has ever dared describe himself as he is.

On the other hand, as far as such a thing is possible, I should like to have been an objective writer. What I call an objective author is one who chooses themes without ever taking himself as the subject. But the modern mania of identifying the author with his subject matter will not allow him this relative creative liberty. Thus does one become a prophet of the absurd. Yet what else have I done except reason about an idea I discovered in the streets of my time? That I have nourished this idea (and part of me nourishes it still) along with my whole generation goes without saying. I simply set it far enough away so that I could deal with it and decide on its logic. Everything that I've been able to write since shows this plainly enough. But it is more convenient to exploit a cliché than a nuance. They've chosen the cliché: so I'm as absurd as ever.

What is the point of saying yet again that in the experience which interested me, and which I happened to write about, the absurd can be considered only as a point of departure—even though the memory and feeling of it still accompany the farther advances. In the same manner, with all due sense of proportion, Cartesian doubt, which is systematic, was not enough to make Descartes a skeptic. In any case, how can one limit oneself to saying that nothing has meaning and that we must plunge into absolute despair? Without getting to the bottom of things, one can at least mention that just as there is no absolute materialism, since merely to form this word is already to acknowledge something in the world apart from matter, there is likewise no total nihilism. The moment you say that everything is nonsense you express something meaningful. Refusing the world all meaning amounts to abolishing all value judgments. But living, and eating, for example, are in themselves value judgments. You choose to remain alive the moment you do not allow yourself to die of hunger, and consequently you recognize that life has at least a relative value. What, in fact, does "literature of despair" mean? Despair is silent. Even silence, moreover, is meaningful if your eyes speak. True despair is the agony of death, the grave or the abyss. If he speaks, if he reasons, above all if he writes, immediately the brother reaches out his hand, the tree is justified, love is born. Literature of despair is a contradiction in terms.

Of course, a certain optimism is not my speciality. Like all men of my age, I grew up to the sound of the drums of the First World War, and our history since that time has remained murder, injustice, or violence. But real pessimism, which does exist, lies in outbidding all this cruelty and shame. For my part, I have never ceased fighting against this dishonor, and I hate only the cruel. I have sought only reasons to transcend our darkest nihilism. Not, I would add, through virtue, nor because of some rare elevation of the spirit, but from an instinctive fidelity to a light in which I was born, and in which for thousands of years men have learned to welcome life even in suffering. Aeschylus is often heartbreaking; yet he radiates light and warmth. At the center of his universe, we find not fleshless nonsense but an enigma, that is to say, a meaning which is difficult to decipher because it dazzles us. Likewise, to the unworthy but nonetheless stubborn sons of Greece who still survive in this emaciated century, the scorching heat of our history may seem unendurable, but they endure it in the last analysis because they want to understand it. In the center of our work, dark though it may be, shines an inexhaustible sun, the same sun that shouts today across the hills and plain.

After this, the flaxen fire can burn; who cares what we appear to be and what we usurp? What we are, what we have to be, are enough to fill our lives and occupy our strength. Paris is a wondrous cave, and its inhabitants, seeing their own shadows reflected on the far wall, take them for the only reality there is. The same is true of the strange, fleeting renown this town dispenses. But we have learned, far from Paris, that there is a light behind us, that we must turn around and cast off our chains in order to face it directly, and that our task before we die is to seek through any words to identify it. Every artist is undoubtedly pursuing his truth. If he is a great artist, each work brings him nearer to it, or, at least, swings still closer toward this center, this buried sun where everything must one day burn. If he is mediocre, each work takes him further from it, the center is then everywhere, the light disintegrates. But the only people who can help the artist in his obstinate quest are those who love him, and those who, themselves lovers or creators, find in their own passion the measure of all passion, and hence know how to criticize.

Yes, all this noise . . . when peace would be to love and create in silence! But we must learn to be patient. One moment more, the sun seals our mouths.

1950

Return to Tipasa

You sailed away from your father's dwelling
With your heart on fire, Medea! And you passed
Between the rocky gates of the seas;
And now you sleep on a foreign shore.

—*Medea*

For five days the rain had been failing unceasingly on Algiers, finally drenching the sea itself. From the heights of an apparently inexhaustible sky, unending sheets of rain, so thick they were viscous, crashed into the gulf. Soft and gray like a great sponge, the sea heaved in the shapeless bay. But the surface of the water seemed almost motionless beneath the steady rain. At long intervals, however, a broad and imperceptible movement raised a murky cloud of steam from the sea and rolled it into the harbor, below a circle of soaking boulevards. The town itself, its white walls running with damp, gave off another cloud of steam that billowed out to meet the first. Whichever way you turned you seemed to be breathing water, you could drink the very air.

Looking at this drowned sea, seeing in December an Algiers that was still for me the city of summers, I walked about and waited. I had fled from the night of Europe, from a winter of faces. But even the town of summers was emptied of its laughter, offering me only hunched and streaming backs. In the evening, in the fiercely lit cafés where I sought refuge, I read my age on faces I recognized without knowing their names. All I knew was that these men had been young when I was, and that now they were young no longer.

I stayed on, though, without any clear idea of what I was waiting for, except, perhaps, the moment when I could go back to Tipasa. It is certainly a great folly, and one that is almost always punished, to go back to the places of one's youth, to want to relive at forty the things one loved or greatly enjoyed at twenty. But I was aware of this folly. I had already been back to Tipasa once, not long after those war years that marked for me the end of my youth. I hoped, I think, to rediscover there a liberty I was unable to forget. Here, more than twenty years ago, I had spent whole mornings wandering among the ruins, breathing the scent of absinthe, warming myself against the stones, discovering the tiny, short-lived roses that survive in springtime. Only at noon, when even the crickets are silenced by the heat, would I flee from the avid blaze of an all-consuming light. Sometimes, at night, I would sleep open-eyed beneath a sky flowing with stars. I was alive at those moments. Fifteen years later, I found my ruins again. A few steps from the first waves, I followed the streets of the forgotten city across the fields covered with bitter trees; and, on the hills overlooking the bay, could still caress their pillars, which were the color of bread. But now the ruins were surrounded by barbed wire, and could be reached only through official entrances. It was also forbidden, for reasons sanctioned, it would seem, by morality, to walk there after dark; by day, one would meet an official guard. That morning, doubtless by chance, it was raining across the whole sweep of the ruins.

Bewildered, walking through the lonely, rain-soaked countryside, I tried at least to recover the strength that has so far never failed me, that helps me to accept what is, once I have realized I cannot change it. I could not, of course, travel backward through time and restore to this world the face I had loved, which had disappeared in a single day a long time before. On the second of September, 1939, I did not go to Greece, as I had planned. Instead, the war enveloped us, then Greece itself. This distance, these years separating the warm ruins from the barbed wire, were also within me, as I stood that day staring at tombs filled with black water or beneath the dripping tamarisk trees. Raised above all in the spectacle of a beauty that was my only wealth, I had begun in plenty. The barbed wire came later—I mean tyrannies, war, policings, the time of revolt. We had had to come to terms with night: the beauty of daytime was only a memory. And in this muddy Tipasa, even the memory was growing dim. No room now for beauty, fullness, or youth! In the light cast by the flames, the world had suddenly shown its wrinkles and its afflictions, old and new. It had suddenly grown old, and we had too. I knew the ardor I had come in search of could only be roused in someone not expecting it. There is no love without a little innocence. Where was innocence? Empires were crumbling, men and nations were tearing at one another's throats; our mouths were dirtied. Innocent at first without knowing it, now we were unintentionally guilty: the more we knew, the greater the mystery. This is why we busied ourselves, oh mockery, with morality. Frail in spirit, I dreamed of virtue! In the days of innocence, I did not know morality existed. Now I knew it did, and could not live up to it. On the promontory I had loved in former days, between the drenched pillars of the ruined temple, I seemed to be walking behind someone whose footsteps I could still hear on the tombstones and mosaics, but whom I would never catch up with again. I went back to Paris, and stayed for some years before returning home again.

During all these years, however, I had a vague feeling of missing something. Once you have had the chance to love intensely, your life is spent in search of the same light and the same ardor. To give up beauty and the sensual happiness that comes with it and devote one's self exclusively to unhappiness requires a nobility I lack. But, after all, nothing is true that compels us to make it exclusive. Isolated beauty ends in grimaces, solitary justice in oppression. Anyone who seeks to serve the one to the exclusion of the other serves no one, not even himself, and in the end is doubly the servant of injustice. A day comes when, because we have been inflexible, nothing amazes us anymore, everything is known, and our life is spent in starting again. It is a time of exile, dry lives, dead souls. To come back to life, we need grace, a homeland, or to forget ourselves. On certain mornings, as we turn a corner, an exquisite dew falls on our heart and then vanishes. But the freshness lingers, and this, always, is what the heart needs. I had to come back once again.

And, in Algiers a second time, still walking under the same downpour that I felt had not stopped since what I thought was my final departure, in the midst of this immense melancholy smelling of rain and sea, in spite of the misty sky, the sight of people's backs fleeing beneath the deluge, the cafés whose sulphurous light decomposed everyone's face, I persisted in my hopes. Anyway, didn't I know that rain in Algiers, although it looks as if it would go on forever, nonetheless does stop suddenly, like the rivers in my country that swell to a flood in two hours, devastate acres of land, and dry up again in an instant? One evening, in fact, the rain stopped. I waited still one more night. A liquid morning rose, dazzling, over the pure sea. From the sky, fresh as a rose, washed and rewashed by the waters, reduced by each successive laundering to its most delicate and clearest texture, a quivering light fell, endowing each house, each tree, with a palpable shape and a magic newness. The earth must have risen in just such a light the morning the world was born. Once again I set out for Tipasa.

There is not a single one of these sixty-nine kilometers of highway that is not filled for me with memories and sensations. A violent childhood, adolescent daydreams to the hum of the bus's engines, mornings, the freshness of young girls, beaches, young muscles always tensed, the slight anguish that the evening brings to a sixteen-year-old heart, the desire to live, glory, and always the same sky, for months on end, with its inexhaustible strength and light, as companion to the years, a sky insatiable, one by one devouring victims lying crucified upon the beach at the funereal hour of noon. Always the same sea as well, almost impalpable in the morning air, glimpsed again on the horizon as soon as the road, leaving the Sahel and its hills with their bronze-colored vineyards, dipped down toward the coast. But I did not stop to look at it. I wanted to see the Chenoua again—that heavy, solid mountain, carved all in one piece and running along the west side of Tipasa Bay before descending into the sea. You see it from far away, long before you get there, as a light blue haze still mingling with the sea. But gradually it condenses as you come nearer, until it takes on the color of the waters surrounding it, like an immense and motionless wave brutally caught in the very act of breaking over a suddenly calm sea. Nearer still, almost at the gates of Tipasa, you see its frowning mass, brown and green, the old, unshakable, moss-covered god, port and haven for its sons, of whom I am one. I was gazing at it as I finally crossed the barbed wire and stood among the ruins. And, in the glorious December light, as happens only once or twice in lives that may later be described as heaped with every blessing, I found exactly what I had come in search of, something which in spite of time and in spite of the world was offered to me and truly to me alone, in this deserted nature. From the olive-strewn forum, one could see the village down below. Not a sound came from it; wisps of smoke rose in the limpid air. The sea also lay silent, as if breathless beneath the unending shower of cold, glittering light. From the Chenoua, a distant cock crow alone sang the fragile glory of the day. Across the ruins, as far as one could see, there were nothing but pitted stones and absinthe plants, trees and perfect columns in the transparence of the crystal air. It was as if the morning stood still, as if the sun had stopped for an immeasurable moment. In this light and silence, years of night and fury melted slowly away. I listened to an almost forgotten sound within myself, as if my heart had long been stopped and was now gently beginning to beat again. And, now awake, I recognized one by one the imperceptible sounds that made up the silence: the *basso continuo* of the birds, the short, light sighing of the sea at the foot of the rocks, the vibration of the trees, the blind song of the columns, the whispering of the absinthe plants, the furtive lizards. I heard all this, and also felt the waves of happiness rising up within me. I felt that I had at last come back to harbor, for a moment at least, and that from now on this moment would never end. But soon afterward the sun rose visibly a degree higher in the sky. A blackbird chirped its brief prelude and immediately, from all around, bird voices exploded with a strength, a jubilation, a joyful discord, an infinite delight. The day moved on. It was to carry me through till evening.

At noon, on the half-sandy slopes, strewn with heliotropes like a foam that the furious waves of the last few days had left behind in their retreat, I gazed at the sea, gently rising and falling as if exhausted, and quenched two thirsts that cannot be long neglected if all one's being is not to dry up, the thirst to love and the thirst to admire. For there is only misfortune in not being loved; there is misery in not loving. All of us, today, are dying of this misery. This is because blood and hatred lay bare the heart itself; the long demand for justice exhausts even the love that gave it birth. In the clamor we live in, love is impossible and justice not enough. That is why Europe hates the daylight and can do nothing but confront one injustice with another. In order to prevent justice from shriveling up, from becoming nothing but a magnificent orange with a dry, bitter pulp, I discovered one must keep a freshness and a source of joy intact within, loving the daylight that injustice leaves unscathed, and returning to the fray with this light as a trophy. Here, once more, I found an ancient beauty, a young sky, and measured my good fortune as I realized at last that in the worst years of our madness the memory of this sky had never left me. It was this that in the end had saved me from despair. I had always known that the ruins of Tipasa were younger than our drydocks or our debris. In Tipasa, the world is born again each day in a light always new. Oh light! The cry of all the characters in classical tragedy who come face to face with their destinies. I knew now that their final refuge was also ours. In the depths of winter, I finally learned that within me there lay an invincible summer.

Once more I left Tipasa, returning to Europe and its struggles. But the memory of that day sustains me still and helps me meet both joy and sorrow with equanimity.

In the difficult times we face, what more can I hope for than the power to exclude nothing and to learn to weave from strands of black and white one rope tautened to the breaking point? In everything I've done or said so far, I seem to recognize these two forces, even when they contradict each other. I have not been able to deny the light into which I was born and yet I have not wished to reject the responsibilities of our time. It would be too easy to set against the gentle name Tipasa other names more sonorous and more cruel: there is, for man today, an inner path that I know well from having traveled both ways upon it, which leads from the summits of the mind to the capitals of crime. And, doubtless, one can always rest, sleep on the hillside or settle into crime. But if we give up a part of what exists, we must ourselves give up being; we must then give up living or loving except by proxy. Thus there is a will to live without refusing anything life offers: the virtue I honor most in this world. From time to time, at least, it's true that I would like to have practiced it. Since few times require to the extent ours does that one be as equal to the best as to the worst, to avoid nothing and keep a double memory alive is precisely what I would like to do. Yes, there is beauty and there are the humiliated. Whatever difficulties the enterprise may present, I would like never to be unfaithful either to the one or the other.

But this still sounds like ethics, and we live for something that transcends ethics. If we could name it, what silence would follow! East of Tipasa, the hill of Sainte-Salsa, evening has come to life. It is still light, of course, but an invisible waning of the light announces the sunset. A wind rises, gentle as the night, and suddenly the untroubled sea chooses its way and flows like a great barren river across the horizon. The sky darkens. Then begins the mystery, the gods of night, and what lies beyond pleasure. But how can this be expressed? The little coin I carry back from here has one clear side, the face of a beautiful woman that reminds me of what I've learned in the course of this day, while the other side, which I feel beneath my fingers homeward bound, has been eaten away. What does this lipless mouth express if not what another, mysterious voice within me says, that daily teaches me my ignorance and my happiness:

The secret I am looking for is buried in a valley of olive trees, beneath the grass and cold violets, around an old house that smells of vines. For more than twenty years I have wandered over this valley, and over others like it, questioning dumb goatherds, knocking at the door of empty ruins. Sometimes, when the first star shines in a still, clear sky, beneath a rain of delicate light, I have thought that I knew. I did know, in fact. Perhaps I still know. But no one is interested in this secret, doubtless I myself do not desire it, and I cannot cut myself off from my own people. I live with my family, who believe they reign over rich and hideous cities, built of stones and mists. Day and night it raises its voice, and everything yields beneath it while it bows down to nothing: it is deaf to all secrets. Its power sustains me and yet bores me, and I come to be weary of its cries. But its unhappiness is my own, we are of the same blood. I too am sick, and am I not a noisy accomplice who has cried out among the stones? Thus I try to forget, I march through our cities of iron and fire, I smile bravely at the night, I welcome the storms, I will be faithful. In fact, I have forgotten: henceforth, I shall be deaf and active. But perhaps one day, when we are ready to die of ignorance and exhaustion, I shall be able to renounce our shrieking tombs, to go and lie down in the valley, under the unchanging light, and learn for one last time what I know.

1953

The Sea Close By

*I grew up with the sea and poverty for me was sumptuous;
then I lost the sea and found all luxuries gray and poverty
unbearable. Since then, I have been waiting. I wait for the
homebound ships, the house of the waters, the limpidity of
day. I wait patiently, am polite with all my strength. I am seen
walking by on fine, sophisticated streets, I admire landscapes, I
applaud like everyone, shake hands, but it is not I who speak.
Men praise me, I dream a little, they insult me, I scarcely show
surprise. Then I forget, and smile at the man who insulted me,
or am too courteous in greeting the person I love. Can I help*

it if all I remember is one image? Finally they summon me to tell them who I am. "Nothing yet, nothing yet . . ."

I surpass myself at funerals. Truly, I excel. I walk slowly through the iron-strewn suburbs, taking the wide lanes planted with cement trees that lead to holes in the cold ground. There, beneath the slightly reddened bandage of the sky, I watch bold workmen inter my friends beneath six feet of earth. If I toss the flower a clay-covered hand holds out to me, it never misses the grave. My piety is exact, my feelings as they should be, my head suitably inclined. I am admired for finding just the right word. But I take no credit: I am waiting.

I have been waiting for a long time. Sometimes, I stumble, I lose my touch, success evades me. What does it matter, I am alone then. I wake up at night, and, still half asleep, think I hear the sound of waves, the breathing of waters. Fully awake, I recognize the wind in the trees and the sad murmur of the empty town. Afterward, all my art is not too much to hide my anguish or clothe it in the prevailing fashion.

At other times, it's the opposite, and I am helped. On certain days in New York, lost at the bottom of those stone and steel shafts where millions of men wander, I would run from one shaft to the next, without seeing where they ended, until, exhausted, I was sustained only by the human mass seeking its way out. But, each time, there was the distant honking of a tugboat to remind me that this empty well of a city was an island, and that off the tip of the Battery the water of my baptism lay in wait for me, black and rotting, covered with hollow corks.

Thus, I who own nothing, who have given away my fortune,

*who camp in all my houses, am still heaped, when I choose,
with every blessing; I can set sail at any hour, a stranger to
despair. There is no country for those who despair, but I know
that the sea precedes and follows me, and I hold my madness
ready. Those who love and are separated can live in grief, but
this is not despair: they know that love exists. This is why I
suffer, dry-eyed, in exile, I am still waiting. A day comes, at
last . . .*

The sailors' bare feet beat softly on the deck. We are setting sail at daybreak. The moment we leave the harbor a
short, gusty wind vigorously brushes the sea, which curls
backward in small, foamless waves. A little later, the wind
freshens and strews the sea with swiftly vanishing camel-
lias. Thus, throughout the morning, we hear our sails slap-
ping above a cheerful pond. The waters are heavy, scaly,
covered with cool froth. From time to time the waves lap
against the bow; a bitter, unctuous foam, the gods' saliva,
flows along the wood and loses itself in the water, where
it scatters into shapes that die and are reborn, the hide of
some white and blue cow, an exhausted beast that floats for
a long time in our wake.

Ever since our departure, the seagulls have been following
our ship, apparently without effort, almost without moving
their wings. Their fine, straight navigation scarcely leans
upon the breeze. Suddenly, a loud plop at the level of the

kitchens stirs up a greedy alarm among the birds, throwing their fine flight into confusion and sending up a fire of white wings. The seagulls whirl madly in every direction and then with no loss of speed drop from the fight one by one and dive toward the sea. A few seconds later they are together again on the water, a quarrelsome farmyard that we leave behind, nesting in the hollow of the wave, slowly picking through the manna of the scraps.

At noon, under a deafening sun, the sea is so exhausted it scarcely finds the strength to rise. When it falls back on itself it makes the silence whistle. After an hour's cooking, the pale water, a vast white-hot iron sheet, sizzles. In a minute it will turn and offer its damp side, now hidden in waves and darkness, to the sun.

We pass the gates of Hercules, the headland where Antaeus died. Beyond, there is ocean everywhere; on one side we pass the Horn and the Cape of Good Hope, the meridians wed the latitudes, the Pacific drinks the Atlantic. At once, setting course for Vancouver, we sail slowly toward the South Seas. A few cable lengths away, Easter Island, Desolation, and the New Hebrides file past us in convoy. Suddenly, one morning, the seagulls disappear. We are far from any land, and alone, with our sails and our engines.

Alone also with the horizon. The waves come from the invisible East, patiently, one by one; they reach us, and then, patiently, set off again for the unknown West, one by one. A long voyage, with no beginning and no end . . . Rivers and streams pass by, the sea passes and remains. This is how one ought to love, faithful and fleeting. I wed the sea.

The high seas. The sun sinks and is swallowed by the fog long before it reaches the horizon. For a brief moment, the sea is pink on one side and blue on the other. Then the waters grow darker. The schooner slides, minute, over the surface of a perfect circle of thick, tarnished metal. And, at the most peaceful hour, as evening comes, hundreds of porpoises emerge from the water, frolic around us for a moment, then flee to the horizon where there are no men. With them gone, silence and the anguish of primitive waters are what remain.

A little later still, we meet an iceberg on the Tropic. Invisible, to be sure, after its long voyage in these warm waters, but still effective: it passes to starboard, where the rigging is briefly covered with a frosty dew, while to port the day dies without moisture.

Night does not fall at sea. It rises, rather, toward the still pale sky, from the depths of waters an already drowned sun gradually darkens with its thick ashes. For a brief moment, Venus shines alone above the black waves. In the twinkling of an eye, stars swarm in the liquid night.

The moon has risen. First it lights the water's surface gently, then climbs higher and inscribes itself in the supple water. At last, at its zenith, it lights a whole corridor of sea, a rich river of milk which, with the motion of the ship, streams down inexhaustibly toward us across the dark ocean. Here is the faithful night, the cool night I called for in the rollicking lights, the alcohol, the tumult of desire.

We sail across spaces so vast they seem unending. Sun and moon rise and fall in turn, on the same thread of light and night. Days at sea, as similar each to the other as happiness …

This life rebellious to forgetfulness, rebellious to memory, that Stevenson speaks of.

Dawn. We sail perpendicularly across the Tropic of Cancer, the waters groan and are convulsed. Day breaks over a surging sea, full of steel spangles. The sky is white with mist and heat, with a dead but unbearable glare, as if the sun had turned liquid in the thickness of the clouds, over the whole expanse of the celestial vault. A sick sky over a decomposing sea. As the day draws on, the heat grows in the white air. All day long, our bow noses out clouds of flying fish, tiny iron birds, forcing them from their hiding places in the waves.

In the afternoon, we meet a steamer bound for home. The salute our foghorns exchange with three great prehistoric hoots, the signals of passengers lost at sea warning there are other humans present, the gradually increasing distance between the two ships, their separation at last on the malevolent waters, all this fills the heart with pain. These stubborn madmen, clinging to planks tossed upon the mane of immense oceans, in pursuit of drifting islands: what man who cherishes solitude and the sea will ever keep himself from loving them?

In the very middle of the Atlantic, we bend beneath the savage winds that blow endlessly from pole to pole. Each cry we utter is lost, flies off into limitless space. But this shout, carried day after day on the winds, will finally reach land at one of the flattened ends of the earth and echo timelessly against the frozen walls until a man, lost somewhere in his shell of snow, hears it and wants to smile with happiness.

I was half asleep in the early afternoon sun when a terrible noise awoke me. I saw the sun in the depths of the sea, the waves reining in the surging heavens. Suddenly, the sea was afire, the sun flowed in long icy draughts down my throat. The sailors laughed and wept around me. They loved, but could not forgive one another. I recognized the world for what it was that day. I decided to accept the fact that its good might at the same time be evil and its transgressions beneficial. I realized that day that there were two truths, and that one of them ought never to be uttered.

The curious austral moon, looking slightly pared, keeps us company for several nights and then slides rapidly from the sky into the sea, which swallows it. The Southern Cross, the infrequent stars, the porous air remain. At the same instant, the wind ceases. The sky rolls and pitches above our immobile masts. Engine dead, sails hove to, we are whistling in the warm night as the water beats amicably against our sides. No commands, the machines are silent. Why indeed should we continue and why return? Our cup runneth over, a mute rapture lulls us invincibly to sleep. There are days like this when all is accomplished; we must let ourselves flow with them, like swimmers who keep on until exhausted. What can we accomplish? I have always concealed it from myself. Oh bitter bed, princely couch, the crown lies at the bottom of the seas.

In the morning, the lukewarm water foams gently under our propeller. We put on speed. Toward noon, traveling from distant continents, a herd of walruses cross our path, overtake us, and swim rhythmically to the north, followed by multicolored birds which from time to time alight upon their tusks. This rustling forest slowly vanishes on the horizon. A little later the sea is covered with strange yellow flowers. Toward evening, for hour after hour, we are preceded by an invisible song. Comfortably, I fall asleep.

All sails stretched to the keen breeze, we skim across a clear and rippling sea. At top speed, our helm goes hard to port. And toward nightfall, correcting our course again, listing so far to starboard that our sails skim the water, we sail rapidly along the side of a southern continent I recognize from having once flown blindly over it in the barbarous coffin of an airplane. I was an idle king and my chariot dawdled; I waited for the sea but it never came. The monster roared, took off from the guano fields of Peru, hurled itself above the beaches of the Pacific, flew over the fractured white vertebrae of the Andes and then above the herds of flies that cover the immense Argentinian plain, linking in one swoop the milk-drowned Uruguayan meadows to Venezuela's black rivers, landing, roaring again, quivering with greed at the sight of new empty spaces to devour, and yet never failing to move forward or at least doing so only with a convulsed, obstinate slowness, a fixed, weary, and intoxicated energy. I felt I was dying in this metallic cell and dreamed of bloodshed and orgies. Without space, there is neither innocence nor liberty! When a man cannot breathe, prison means death or madness; what can he do there but kill and possess? But today I have all the air I need, all our sails slap in the blue air, I am going to shout at the speed, we'll toss our sextants and compasses into the sea.

Our sails are like iron under the imperious wind. The coast drifts at full speed before our eyes, forests of royal coconut trees whose feet are bathed by emerald lagoons, a quiet bay, full of red sails, moonlit beaches. Great buildings loom up, already cracking under the pressure of the virgin forest that begins in the back yards; here and there a yellow ipecac or a tree with violet branches bursts through a window; Rio finally crumbles away behind us and the monkeys of the Tijuca will laugh and gibber in the vegetation that will cover its new ruins. Faster still, along wide beaches where the waves spread out in sheaves of sand, faster still, where the Uruguayan sheep wade into the sea and instantly turn it yellow. Then, on the Argentinian coast, great coarse heaps of burning kindling, set up at regular intervals, raise slowly grilling halves of oxen to the sky. At night, the ice from Tierra del Fuego comes and beats for hours against our hull, the ship hardly loses speed and tacks about. In the morning, the single wave of the Pacific, whose cold foam boils green and white for thousands of kilometers along the Chilean coast, slowly lifts us up and threatens to wreck us. The helm avoids it, overtakes the Kerguelen Islands. In the sweetish evening the first Malayan boats come out to meet us.

"To sea! To sea!" shouted the marvelous boys in one of the books from my childhood. I have forgotten everything about that book except this cry. "To sea!", and across the Indian Ocean into the corridor of the Red Sea, where on silent nights one can hear the desert stones, scorched in the daytime, freeze and crack one by one as we return to the ancient sea in which all cries are hushed.

Finally, one morning, we drop anchor in a bay filled with a strange silence, beaconed with fixed sails. A few sea birds are quarrelling in the sky over scraps of reeds. We swim ashore to an empty beach; all day plunging into the water and drying off on the sand. When evening comes, under a sky that turns green and fades into the distance, the sea, already calm, grows more peaceful still. Short waves shower vaporous foam on the lukewarm shore. The sea birds have disappeared. All that is left is space, open to a motionless voyage.

Knowing that certain nights whose sweetness lingers will keep returning to the earth and sea after we are gone, yes, this helps us die. Great sea, ever in motion, ever virgin, my religion along with night! It washes and satiates us in its sterile billows, frees us and holds us upright. Each breaker brings its promise, always the same. What does each say? If I were to die surrounded by cold mountains, ignored by the world, an outcast, at the end of my strength, at the final moment the sea would flood my cell, would lift me above myself and help me die without hatred.

At midnight, alone on the shore. A moment more, and I shall set sail. The sky itself has weighed anchor, with all its stars, like the ships covered with lights which at this very hour throughout the world illuminate dark harbors. Space and silence weigh equally upon the heart. A sudden love, a great work, a decisive act, a thought that transfigures, all these at certain moments bring the same unbearable anxiety, quickened with an irresistible charm. Living like this, in the delicious anguish of being, in exquisite proximity to a danger whose name we do not know, is this the same as rushing to our doom? Once again, without respite, let us race to our destruction.

I have always felt I lived on the high seas, threatened, at the heart of a royal happiness.

1953

Notes

xi   **"If ... I never manage to rewrite":** In 1958, when Camus wrote this preface, he was indeed rewriting *The Wrong Side and the Right Side* as he drafted *The First Man*, with its scenes from Camus's childhood in Algiers. The novel, unfinished at Camus's death in 1960, was published to great acclaim in 1995.

1   **to Jean Grenier:** Jean Grenier (1898–1971) was Camus's philosophy teacher at the Algiers Lycée and later at the University of Algiers. In 1936, he directed Camus's thesis for the equivalent of a master's degree, titled "Christian Metaphysics and Neoplatonism."

4   **Brice Parain often maintains:** Brice Parain (1897–1971), philosopher and writer, Camus's fellow editor and friend at Gallimard.

6   **as Chamfort would put it:** Nicolas Chamfort (1741–1794), a French writer known for his aphorisms. Camus wrote an introduction to Chamfort's *Maxims* (1944).

10   **The ambitions of a Lucien de Rubempré or a Julien Sorel:** A reference to the heroes of Balzac's *Lost Illusions* and Stendhal's *The Red and the Black*—both characters suffer from great, failed ambitions.

11   **dispense as generously as Pernod:** Pernod, an anise-flavored alcoholic drink, popular in colonial Algeria.

36 **The perfect song of a *derbouka*:** A percussive instrument in the Arab-Muslim musical tradition; known in English as a goblet drum.

86 **to Jacques Heurgon:** Jacques Heurgon was a literature professor at the University of Algiers who founded the short-lived review *Rivages*, where Camus published an excerpt from "Summer in Algiers" in February–March 1939.

88 **In Belcourt and Bab-el-Oued, old men sitting:** Working-class neighborhoods of central Algiers. Camus grew up in Belcourt on the rue de Lyon (now the rue Belouizdad).

89 **a pattern of white cubes, the Casbah:** The old city of Algiers, built into the hillside, whose steep alleys and Ottoman-era white stucco houses were home to a diverse population of Kabyle, Arab, and Jewish natives. The life of the Casbah has animated countless films and books, most famously the French feature film *Pépé le Moko* (1937) and its American remake, *Algiers* (1938).

91 **The dance hall at Padovani Beach:** A popular beach bathhouse and dance hall in central Algiers along the waterfront. This would have been "the public beach down at the harbor" where Meursault took Marie in *The Stranger*.

94 **the cemetery on the boulevard Bru:** One of two European cemeteries in the city, overlooking Belcourt and the Bay of Algiers (today: Cimetière El Madania on the Boulevard des Martyrs). Camus's mother, Catherine Sintès Camus, is buried here.

97 **the unity Plotinus longed for:** Camus was drawing here on his master's thesis at the University of Algiers, "Christian Metaphysics and Neoplatonism" (1936), his study of two ancient North African theologians, Augustine and Plotinus.

117 **to Pierre Galindo:** Galindo was Camus's friend in Algeria before the war. Later, he moved to Paris and took a nominal job at Camus's newspaper, *Combat*. Camus liked to quip that his oddball, taciturn friend was one of the models for Meursault in *The Stranger*.

119 **"It's between the two of us now":** A reference to the famous last scene of Balzac's *Old Man Goriot*, where the ambitious young Eugène de Rastignac stares down at the city he plans to conquer. "A nous deux" is a fencing term; the phrase has also been translated as "Now let us fight it out!"

120 **In Oran, you meet Gogol's Klestakoff:** A reference to the corrupt civil servant in Gogol's satiric play *The Government Inspector* (1836).

121 **You can find in Oran:** Observations of life in Oran appear in Camus's November 1939, February 1940, and January–March 1941 notebooks.

125 **Santa Cruz carved out of the rock:** Santa Cruz refers both to the Spanish fort high above the Bay of Oran and to the chapel just below it.

129 **grinds out Tino Rossi:** Tino Rossi (1907–1983) was a popular Corsican singer whose career took off in 1933.

135 **Their creator was named Caïn:** Auguste Caïn (1821–1894) sculpted the lions in front of the city hall of Oran on the Place d'Armes. In *The Plague*, Tarrou keeps a notebook where he describes the bronze animals in great detail. In his own March 1941 notebook, Camus derides "the insignificant unknown who sculpted the insignificant lions."

138 **But Le Poittevin died:** Flaubert writes about the last words of his friend Alfred Le Poittevin. The anecdote appears in Camus's notebooks from March 1940.

139 **in the direction of Canastel:** A favorite tourist spot of cliffs and forest overlooking the Mediterranean in the eastern district of Oran.

153 **perched high on a rock above the Rummel Gorges:** Constantine, a city in northeastern Algeria, perches over the deep Rummel Gorge or ravine, its districts linked by bridges. Rummel Gorge also refers to the much photographed natural rock bridge that rises two hundred feet from the bottom of the ravine.

156 **As for the picturesque:** The Village Nègre of Oran refers to the neighborhood where the native population lived after they were pushed out of the center of the city.

166 **Everything grows quiet beneath its force, and Mount Luberon:** The Luberon is a mountain range in the Vaucluse (Provence). After World War II, Camus visited the region frequently and spent time there with his friend the poet René Char in the Provençal town of L'Isle sur la Sorgue. In 1958, Camus bought a home in nearby Lourmarin at the foot of the mountain, where he is buried today. "The Enigma," dedicated to Char, was composed in 1950.

180 **I wanted to see the Chenoua again:** A mountain range on the Mediterranean coast of Algeria between Tipasa and Cherchell.

186 **The Sea Close By:** First published in 1954 in *La Nouvelle Revue Française*, "The Sea Close By" draws on Camus's two transatlantic voyages to the Americas. He crossed from Le Havre to New York in March 1946 and from Marseille to Dakar to Rio de Janeiro in July 1949. The essay is mostly inspired by the second crossing.